D1643876

Below Stairs in the Great Country Houses

ADELINE HARTCUP

SIDGWICK & JACKSON
LONDON

First published in Great Britain in 1980
by Sidgwick and Jackson Limited
Copyright © 1980 Adeline Hartcup

Line drawings by Douglas Lyndon-Skeggs
Picture research by Libby Joy

ISBN 0 283 98695 6

Printed in Great Britain by
R. J. Acford, Industrial Estate, Chichester, Sussex
for Sidgwick and Jackson Limited
1 Tavistock Chambers, Bloomsbury Way
London WC1A 2SG
Phototypesetting by Swiftpages Limited, Liverpool

For John
who suggested the subject

Contents

Acknowledgements

Much of the subject-matter of this book was discovered during a long and exhilarating treasure-hunt through nineteenth-century memoirs, diaries, letters, and biographies. These are listed in the bibliography. Novels written at, or about, the same time yielded a surprisingly thin harvest, though everyone remembers the housekeeper in *Pride and Prejudice*, who showed Elizabeth Bennet and her uncle and aunt round Pemberley, which is almost certainly Chatsworth. And Thackeray's Berkeley Square footman, Charles James Yellowplush (alias C. Jeames de la Pluche, Esq.) provides some appetizing crumbs from the servants' hall table. But most nineteenth-century novelists took for granted the servants and the daily workings of the great houses they described. They introduce us to the Duke of Omnium, to Sir Leicester Dedlock, Harry Coningsby, Lord Ormont, and Lord Mountfalcon, but it never occurs to them that we would also like to hear about goings-on behind the green baize door and below the marble stairs.

Most of my material has never been published before and comes from the great houses themselves. Their muniment rooms are sometimes deep down in the basement (Hatfield and Chatsworth), sometimes in a tower at the top of a winding staircase (Holkham), sometimes in a lodge just inside the gates (Wilton). The Woburn archives are housed at the Bedford Office in London, and those from Petworth and Attingham are boarded out for safe keeping with their County Record Offices.

It was a privilege and a pleasure to be allowed to browse among these historic papers. Learned and kindly archivists added their enthusiasm to mine and brought out giant leather-bound wage books and ledgers, letters, diaries, newspaper cuttings, inventories, bills, invitations, and photograph albums. To them and to the owners of the houses I am deeply grateful. Access to the archives of the houses I have described was allowed by kind permission of the Earl of Leicester, the Marquess of Salisbury, Rt Hon. Lord Egremont, the Earl of Pembroke, the Duke of Bedford and the Trustees of the Bedford Estates, the National Trust, the Shropshire County Record

ACKNOWLEDGEMENTS

Office and Duke of Devonshire and the Trustees of the Chatsworth Settlement. I had valuable help from Dr W.O. Hassall, Lord Leicester's Librarian; Mr R.H. Harcourt Williams, Librarian and Archivist to the Marquess of Salisbury; Mrs P. Gill, County Archivist of West Sussex; Mr R.H. Mellish, of the Wilton Estate Office; Mrs M.P.G. Draper, Archivist at the Bedford Office; Mr J.M. Collinson, Archivist of Leeds City Archives Department; and Mr Peter Day, Librarian of the Devonshire Collections.

Although there is no separate chapter on Longleat or Knole, I was kindly allowed to work on the Longleat archives by the Marquess of Bath and was warmly welcomed there by his Librarian and Archivist, Miss B.M. Austin; and I was taken on a fascinating tour of the kitchens, and of the servants' bedrooms in the attics and garrets of Knole by Mr Hugh Sackville-West.

I suppose the book could have been written without the help of the London Library and my husband, but I am thankful that I did not have to make the attempt.

Swanton, December 1979   A.H.

List of Illustrations

LIST OF ILLUSTRATIONS

PART ONE

How the Houses Were Run

1

Below the Marble Stairs

The preposterous pace of flunkeydom in the stateliest of the great houses had already slowed down a little by the first years of the nineteenth century. Gone were the days described by Horace Walpole when a guest at Woburn Abbey dropped a silver piece on the floor and said, 'Oh, never mind; let the Groom of the Chambers have it', only to be corrected by the Duchess of Bedford, 'Let the carpet-sweeper have it; the Groom of the Chambers never takes anything but gold.'

But armies of servants were still employed in the stately homes. At Ashridge the Duke of Bridgewater had five hundred men working for him in his gardens, conservatories and workshops, and never refused a job to a local man. He almost doubled his pay-list – from five hundred to eight hundred – during bad times of unemployment and poverty. In some houses there were ten or more sitting-rooms for the servants, who checked in to each according to the social standing of their jobs. In 1816 Joseph Farington, the painter and R.A., whose diary is today as fascinating as his pictures are boring, found Lord Fitzwilliam's mansion at Wentworth 'princely in all respects'. Seventy sat down to dinner every day in the servants' hall, while thirty upper servants took their meal in the more refined seclusion of the housekeeper's room.

By then the bad times were beginning, and thousands of livery servants lost their jobs. Others had their pay docked by as much as fifteen per cent, were paid in pounds instead of guineas, or were allowed only two instead of three suits of livery each year. But by the middle of the century England was the richest and most vigorous nation in the world. Agriculture, still the country's chief industry, was managed from the great rural estates, and their success and prosperity were reflected in the splendour of their owners' houses.

But for all their splendour, the houses were often very uncomfortable. Vast rooms and fireless corridors were almost impossible to heat in winter, and one guest found Woburn so chilly in July that he wore his hat at breakfast, explaining that he was afraid that without it he would catch cold. Thomas Creevey, another great diarist of political and social life during the first thirty years of the century, described an equally cheerless meal at Knowsley in December 1822. The new dining-room there measured fifty-three feet by thirty-seven, and in spite of the heat from two blazing fires, thirty-six wax candles above the table and fourteen on it, not to mention ten great lamps on tall pedestals round the room, 'those at the bottom of the table said it was quite petrifying in that neighbourhood, and the report here is that they have since been obliged to abandon it entirely from the cold'.

Other houses were just as icy. Disraeli's visit to Longleat was a disaster, though his hosts made great efforts to make him comfortable. A temporary lavatory was even contrived for him in his bedroom, but he was wretched, felt very cold, and grumbled that he found it difficult to get any ink. Politicians seem to have been specially unfortunate on their visits to country houses. Sir Robert Peel wrote to his wife in 1833 about the misery of life in winter at Apethorpe, Lord Westmorland's house, which was as big as one of the smaller Oxford colleges, with bedrooms about a quarter of a mile from the billiard room and the drawing-room. There was no fire because their host was terrified of the house burning down, spiders and rats inhabited the closet, and Peel's candle had blown out half-way, as he put it, to this paradise.

Masters and Men

In summer or winter, on state occasions or when vast rooms lay empty and unlit, the heart of the house was the servants' hall. From there the life-blood of the household was carried to every room and staircase, and to the various outside departments, by the hard-working team of servants. Theirs was a society with as many, and as rigid, social castes as the one it served, with clearly defined and accepted rules, and with a place and a job for each of its members. Everyone could be certain of a roof over his head, clothes to wear, and food to eat in times when such necessities were not always easy to come by in the hard world beyond the park gates. There is surprisingly little evidence of discontent or rebellion, probably because those who did not accept the established order would either not look for work in a noble house, or would soon be shown the door if they did not fit in below stairs.

And the servants' grievances were not likely to come to the notice of writers of memoirs or letters.

But sometimes things did go wrong. In 1810 the unpopular Duke of Cumberland, George III's son, was attacked and nearly murdered by his valet, and thirty years later a Swiss manservant found old Lord William Russell so cantankerous and hard to please that he seized a knife from the sideboard and cut his master's throat while he lay asleep. Creevey describes a case of fisticuffs between a spirited servant and his master, the future Lord Durham (who was nicknamed 'King Jog' because of his famous admission that it was possible to 'jog along on £40,000 a year'). Emerging from the hazard room – hazard was a complicated game of dice – at his home after midnight on one occasion in 1824, he was indignant to find no drinking-water, so he began 'belabouring the bell' with such violence that Creevey felt sure the whole contraption would come crashing down. For a long time no one turned up, but at last King Jog's manservant arrived, with some words of explanation which infuriated his master so much that he seized a stick and whacked him twice. The servant, we are happy to read, said he would not put up with such treatment and that if his master hit him again he would be 'obliged to knock him down'. At that King Jog held off, and the affair was ended by the man giving in his notice.

Creevey also tells a less conclusive story of a French maid who was found crying bitterly outside her lady's room after midnight. She gave as her reason that she had had a cruel beating from her mistress. When another maid was sent to give her sal volatile, she was accused of shamming and was not allowed to take it. There must have been little hope of justice on such occasions. Servants who gave or were given notice to leave must often have gone short of a fair 'character', and without that it was not easy to find another job.

Fortunately feelings were usually less violent. When Coke of Norfolk inherited Holkham, he had trouble in getting rid of a land steward who was taking bribes, so for many years he decided to do all that side of the business himself instead of replacing him. Coke's way of solving the problem was a characteristically independent one. It was shared by the Duke of Wellington, who said that the presence of a crowd of idle, officious fellows annoyed him more than he could say, so he brushed his own clothes and regretted that he had not time to clean his boots as well. It was less easy for an old man like Lord Melbourne who, in his later years, knew that the sixteen servants in

'Oh ah! let 'em ring again!', a cartoon by George Cruikshank. A rare moment of rebellion below stairs

The silver road to the dining room

his London home were all 'thievish and drunk' while their master had not the energy to check their accounts, let alone confront them.

Some of the more eccentric noblemen of the day shared Lord Melbourne's dislike of servants and went to extreme lengths to avoid having to come face to face with them. In many houses the maids had to get their above-stairs work done during the morning so that the family and their guests were sure not to meet them afterwards. The tenth Duke of Bedford went even further, and any maid who was seen by him at Woburn was likely to be dismissed. At Crewe Hall house-maids were seen only in chapel, and if they were ever unfortunate enough to be sighted in the house by a visitor they were ordered to leave at once.

One of the oddest of all nineteenth-century peers was the fifth Duke of Portland, who constructed vast underground state rooms and living-rooms for himself at Welbeck Abbey. If he felt like taking an evening walk he would get a woman servant to go forty yards ahead of him with a lantern to light him on his way but with strict instructions not to speak to her master. When he arrived at his town house in Cavendish Square further orders were given to make sure that no servants were in sight. The Duke died in 1879, but Welbeck servants had unusual treatment up to the end of the century. There was a skating-rink in the grounds then, and the sixth Duke avoided the nuisance of seeing housemaids about the place by ordering them to go out and skate if he came across them while they were doing the housework.

One way and another, livery servants had a strenuous time of it at Welbeck. The Duchess was anxious that her footmen, who had generous beer allowances, should not get too plump, so she presented each of them with a bicycle and a set of golf clubs and gave orders that they should take plenty of exercise. She even enlisted the services of a small but agile Japanese judoist, who spent many triumphant hours tossing tall, muscular flunkeys round the Welbeck gymnasium.

Servants had to get used to their masters' whims. The first Marquess of Abercorn could not bear the idea of dirty hands touching his fine linen sheets, so he insisted on his housemaids putting on white kid gloves before they made his bed. In some houses meals had to be served exactly on time. One of the hardest taskmasters on this point was the bachelor eighth Duke of Bedford, who was something of a hypochondriac as well as a recluse, and was convinced that 'waiting

A Fête at Petworth, by F. Witherington, 1835. The day ten thousand guests ate a thousand plum puddings

Inset: The indoor and outdoor servants line up to welcome a guest. George Du Maurier in *Graphic*, 1888

five minutes for a meal after my stomach is prepared for it' upset the whole balance of his mind as well as his body. Sometimes such pernicketiness affected guests as well as servants. The Duke of Wellington forbade his gentlemen visitors to smoke until the ladies had retired to bed. Then they had to take their cigars to the servants' hall, where everything was ready for them, and there the eminent soldiers, politicians, and ambassadors would sit on hard, well-scrubbed wooden chairs, smoking and chatting until their backs ached and they retreated to the comfort of their elegant bedrooms.

But there are plenty of accounts of excellent relations between employers, who felt themselves responsible for the well-being of their staff, and servants, who accepted their situation unquestioningly and loyally worked until they could toil no more. Many servants felt that they were a part of the house, even members of the family. At Warwick Castle the old housekeeper was famous for her devotion to the family, and when she died she left its younger members £20,000, which had been given her over the years by visitors to the castle. The Duke of Wellington, as we have seen, was irritated when servants were inefficient or got in his way, but he would not allow himself to blame them unfairly and had his own method of apologizing when this happened. He would send for the servant he had wronged, ask him a question, and then courteously say, 'Thank you, I am much obliged to you.' It would then be understood that the great man had made his excuses.

Of course one of the main advantages of 'going into service' in a great house was the training it offered at a time when this was impossible to come by – specially for women – elsewhere. Mary Russell Mitford, whose books give a good picture of village and country life during the first half of the century, describes how farmers' daughters went 'into service at the great house at 14, and stayed till they married, learning there, lessons of neatness, domestic skill and respect for quality of all kinds'. Perhaps some of the training might not be much use in everyday life outside an aristocratic home. For instance, the skills a footman reckoned he had learned at Longleat included how to clean silver, how to welcome guests and valet them, how to seem not to listen to his masters' conversation, and how to put rugs around ladies' legs.

Charles Greville, another great memoir-writer of the time, who was friendly with politicians of both parties and a welcome guest at most of their homes, saw both the pros and cons of the situation, and decided in favour of the feudal, paternal set-up. He was at Belvoir Castle on the Duke of Rutland's birthday in 1838, and described how the family and their guests went to the servants' hall,

> where one hundred and forty five had just done dinner and were drinking the Duke's health, singing and speechifying with vociferous applause, shouting, and clapping of hands ... I should like to bring the surly Radical here who scowls and snarls at the selfish aristocracy who have no sympathies with the people, and when he has seen these hundreds feasting in the Castle, and heard their loud shouts of joy and congratulation, and then visited the villages around, and listened to the bells chiming all about the vale, say whether, 'the greatest happiness of the greatest number' would be promoted by the destruction of all the feudality which belongs inseparably to this scene, and by the substitution of some abstract political rights for all the beef and ale and music and dancing with which they are made merry and glad even for so brief a space. The Duke of Rutland is as selfish a man as any of his class – that is, He never does what he does not like, and spends his whole life in a round of such pleasures as suit his taste, but he is neither a foolish nor a bad man, and partly from a sense of duty, partly from inclination, he devotes time and labour to the interest and welfare of the people who live and labour on his estate.

The Rules of the Game

In most houses there were annual servants' balls, when what Mr Mantalini, in Dickens's *Nicholas Nickleby*, called the 'demd horrid grind' of the year's work was rewarded by a splurge of lavish splendour on a scale which at other times was well outside everyone's reach. At Welbeck at Christmas the head footmen were handed envelopes with the Portland crest on the wax seals and five-pound notes inside. Christmas entertaining meant extra hard work for all the staff, but none of them lifted a finger at the magnificent ball for twelve hundred which was given on Twelfth Night in the vast underground ballroom and the three palatial reception rooms, all decorated as for a state occasion. This time the servants, the tenants and their families, and the local tradesmen and their wives were the guests, and fifty waiters were brought in to look after them. An orchestra from London played throughout the evening and the Duchess, in sparkling jewels and a sumptuous dress, opened the ball with the steward as her partner. All the servants were in ball dress, the head housemaid in velvet, the housekeeper in low-necked blue satin, and the Duke and Duchess tactfully drove away early the following morning.

At Longleat the staff had their party on Christmas Day, with presents of dress material for the women and starched collars for the men. Festivities began with dancing in the courtyard, followed by carol-singing, hand-bell ringing, and an entertainment from the mummers. After a great dinner in the servants' hall the fiddlers arrived, and the ball was opened by the Marquess of Bath dancing with the housekeeper, while the butler partnered the Marchioness.

These were the festive high-spots of the year. At other times accepted formalities must have made life simpler for young servants, who had been recruited from country farmhouses or crowded industrial towns and were understandably bewildered by their stately surroundings. The main guide-line was the clear-cut below-stairs social hierarchy, with the 'upper servants' keeping themselves very much to themselves, and a rigid caste system which reflected that of their employers. The upper servants were the house steward, housekeeper, wine butler, under-butler, groom of the chambers, valet, head housemaid and lady's maid. They were also known as the Upper Ten, just as the lower servants were known as the Lower Five, though there were not ten of the one nor five of the other group. The two did not mix socially except in the annual melting-pot of the servants' ball at Christmas. The Upper Ten had their meals in the élite seclusion of the steward's room and were waited upon by the steward's room footman, while the Lower Five ate in the hurly-burly of the servants' hall, served by the hall porter and hall boys. At Welbeck at the end of the century the Upper Ten had wine with their meals, were served on fine china and glass, and each day were given clean napkins in silver rings. At the late supper for the staff, smoking jackets were worn by the men and dress blouses by the women. The Lower Five did without such refinements and drank beer with their meals.

The protocol varied from house to house, but the upper servants' dining-room, whether it was the steward's or the housekeeper's room, was usually known as Pug's Parlour. (A 'pug' was an upper servant in a large establishment.) The housekeeper, even if she was not married, was always addressed as Mrs, just as the butler was respectfully called

Mr by the lower servants. The family and their guests called him by his surname, distinguishing him from the footmen who were called by their Christian names. The lower servants, women as well as men, were addressed unceremoniously by surnames.

In most houses the upper servants honoured the servants' hall with their company for the first half of dinner, entering formally in procession in strict order of precedence while the lower servants stood in respectful silence. Then the housekeeper took the head of the long table, with the cook on her right, the lady's maid on her left, and the other women in gradually descending order on either side of the feminine end of the table. Opposite would be the steward or butler with the under-butler on his right, the coachman on his left and a corresponding masculine diminuendo of dignity until the youngest and humblest of both sexes elbowed each other democratically in the middle. Grace was said by the most eminent person present, then came the meat course, after which the Upper Ten retired to Pug's Parlour – often carrying their china and glass with them – for pudding, cheese, and refined conversation.

Sometimes the withdrawal of the upper servants was accompanied by the strange ritual of 'sinking the beer'. The Upper Ten would have the remains of their servants' hall beer in their glasses when they left the room, and would tip this into the sink as they passed on their way to Pug's Parlour. That was no place for such plebeian tipple, so they would then enjoy a glass – a different one, it is to be hoped – of claret or sherry.

At Longleat the procedure at the end of the last century was for luncheon in the servants' hall to be announced by a hand-bell rung by the odd man. The under servants then took their place at the table and stood there while the upper servants processed in, arm-in-arm, from the steward's room where they had forgathered. The butler and the housekeeper led the way and were followed by the lady's maids, valets, and the groom of the chambers. At a sign from the butler there was a scraping of chairs and they all sat down. The meat course was then served, and when the steward's room boy cleared it away he was followed out of the room by the upper servants in their same procession. They took the rest of their meal in the steward's room and the ceremony ended with a visit to the housekeeper's room for a cup of tea or coffee.

Just as important as the stratification of the household staff was the recognition of correct precedence for visiting servants, who enjoyed the rank of their employers. When there was a distinguished house-party with guests who brought numbers of their own servants, the size and ceremony of the staff dinner mimicked that of the dining-room upstairs. The steward led the way in to the meal, with the highest-ranking of the visiting womenservants – usually a lady's maid – on his arm. The housekeeper followed with her partner – usually a valet – and the other couples came along behind. Evening dress was worn, and visiting staff who had come without this risked being exiled to the informality of the lower servants' room. On some occasions a valet would avoid this disaster by borrowing one of his master's suits.

The difficulty of remembering all the names of visiting servants was solved by calling them after their employers. The grand-daughter of Coke of Norfolk was amused to hear one manservant call out to another, 'I say, Stanhope, did you clean Rosebery's boots?' And servants who inherited the rank and name of their employers came to be credited with some of their other characteristics as well. Farington describes a visit paid by Lady Holland to Lord Oxford, when she and her servants all made themselves unpopular. 'At dinner she had a foreigner a Servant standing behind Her Chair who tasted what came from each dish that she called, for, & set it before Her or not as He conceived she wd., or not approve its quality.—Her bed was made by two of Her *Men servants* as she sd. our women do not know how to make a bed.' No wonder Lord Oxford's servants did not find such behaviour endearing.

The need for servants to sink their identity in that of their employers was just a part of the job and does not seem to have been resented. In some houses the first footman was always called John, the second footman would be James, and the third footman might be Charles, to save the family the trouble of remembering actual names of staff who came and went, and perhaps had less acceptable names of their own.

Sometimes deeper emotions were involved. Even before Queen Victoria set the nation a lugubrious example with her long-term grief for the Prince Consort, the nineteenth century was a great time for mourning. When there had been a death in one of the families the servants joined their employers in wearing mourning and doing without public entertainments or social festivities. Sex was another taboo. Families were known to get rid of particularly pretty maid-servants when their sons reached an age when such sights began to interest them. When servants fell in love and wanted to marry they were likely to be dismissed by way of a wedding present, though exceptionally liberal families like the Carlisles of Castle Howard celebrated their cook's wedding and gave her an affectionate send-off. But even *they* punished a sixteen-year-old pantry boy who was found flirting and larking with an even younger housemaid by packing him summarily off to his home.

Some jobs were for unmarried servants only. Butlers were expected to be bachelors, mainly because it could be tempting to take home wine and food to wives and children. And a society which accepted an employer's right to control the personal lives of his servants did not hesitate to insist on attendance at church services and household prayers. But there was no nonsense about all being equal within the Church's gate. Lord David Cecil remembers that at Hatfield the servants attended the short morning service in the Chapel at nine o'clock each day, as well as Evensong on Sundays. The upper servants sat in the pew, with the under servants in the rows in front of them. And the congregation was divided off, not only upper from lower servants, and masters from staff, but also men from women. All the men – masters, guests, and servants – sat on the left-hand side of the Chapel, while the women were all seated on the right.

When the Queen and the Prince Consort were at Balmoral their servants always went to church with them, but they had to sit in their own pews, away from the Royal Family, and of course they wore uniform. At other church services, servants in livery usually sat apart from the rest of the congregation, sometimes up in the gallery, which might mean that they were unable to come down and receive the sacrament.

Such contrasts in the way servants were treated reflected contemporary extremes of Whiggery and Toryism and must have been hard to reconcile. The journalists were quick to pounce. When the Prince Regent genially joined in the festivities at a supper party for his servants at the Pavilion at Brighton he was attacked by the Tory press for associating with 'cooks, scullions, dish-washers, lick-trenchers, shoe-blacks, cinder-shifters, candle-snuffers' and such-like riff-raff. But the mud slingers did not change things, and royal as well as other employers went on enjoying time off in their servants' company. In 1845, Queen Victoria visited the Duke of Wellington at Stratfield Saye and the royal party were taken to the famous tennis court, where they

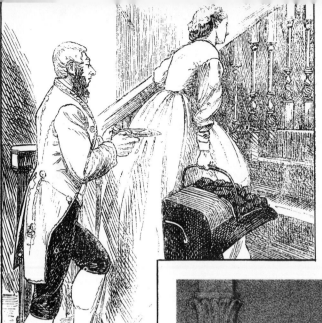

A footman carries a letter upstairs, whilst a maid struggles with the coal. An example of the strict hierarchy below stairs. George Du Maurier in *London Society*, 1863

A footman snatches a quick kiss from a maid on the stairs. Dismissal was often the wedding present for servants who fell in love

watched a game between the Duke's son and two of his staff. The Queen described the occasion in her diary. 'We then all went over to the Tennis Court & saw a very fine game played between Ld. Charles, the Duke's marker, & a fat man called Philips, the Duke's butler, who plays beautifully.' It is a warmer picture to set against the apartheid of the two prim groups from Balmoral at the Sunday church service. And Philips was playing tennis because he enjoyed it and not, as would have been the case at Welbeck, so that he could lose a few inches and look more elegant in the Duke's livery.

Perks, Tips, and Beer Money

Servants certainly lived well in most of the great houses. The account books list vast amounts of food and drink consumed below stairs. Sometimes as much as a pound and a half of meat was each person's daily allowance, with a pound of tea and four pounds of sugar handed out every month by the housekeeper. There was plenty of beer, home-brewed by the butler, at all meals – usually a pint for each manservant at lunch, dinner and supper, while the women were satisfied with half a pint at lunch and supper. Those who did not want beer had beer-money instead. At Hatfield at the turn of the century the housemaids each had two shillings beer-money and as much again in washing-money. They also did well in board wages, which were usually paid when the family was away and the servants catered for themselves.

Perks (from 'perquisites') were another matter. Some were traditional and unquestioned, like the cook's right to bones, dripping, and other fat, which were his or hers to sell for what could be got for them. The lady's maid could be sure of elegant cast-offs from her mistress's wardrobe, and the whole of this – apart from lace, fur, velvet, and satin – usually went to her if her mistress happened to die while she was in her service. Candle-ends and empty bottles were the butler's perks, and by selling them he cleared them out of the way and made himself a welcome shilling or two. The coachman was usually given old wheels from the carriages, though there was an odd proviso that he was given them only if he had been in the family's service at least as long as the wheels.

In many houses there were also good tips to be picked up. Some were given by tradesmen wanting to ingratiate themselves with servants who had the ordering of household supplies. Others went to the porter, or to the housekeeper, who showed casual visitors round the rooms. Gamekeepers were also worth tipping as they made the important decisions about the placing of guns, and were the commanding officers at the great *battues*. (These occurred on autumn and winter mornings, when game was driven by beaters towards a shooting-party. The word – from the French *battre* – and the custom are first found in England during the first years of the nineteenth century.) The head keeper could expect a sovereign for a good day's partridge shooting, and two guineas if they were going for pheasants. There was also the costly ritual of 'vails', a relic of the eighteenth century, when the servants lined up inescapably by the front door so that parting guests could not avoid tipping each as they passed. The practice gradually died out and was given a vigorous push on its way by the Duke of Bedford, who forbade his servants to take tips and dismissed any who disobeyed him. Notices round Woburn proclaimed that the staff were paid high wages 'to work, not to beg'. But in spite of these, one visitor got the impression, as the moment of parting drew near, that several of the servants 'seemed to linger in expectation'.

On and Off the Books

It was usually the house steward's job to engage and dismiss staff – except for personal servants like valets, lady's maids, and nurses, who would be interviewed by the master or mistress they were going to work for. Junior staff were often recruited from the tenantry and village, while more responsible jobs were filled by personal recommendation from other employers, by advertising in the press, and through registry offices. When a likely applicant was discovered, a letter would be sent to his present employer requesting a detailed description or 'character'. A house steward whose working life began in the last century has listed the questions that should be asked about an applicant for the post of lady's maid in a great household:

Is she thoroughly trustworthy, sober and honest?
Is she quick and obliging and kind in illness?
Is she a handy dressmaker, blouse maker and renovator, a careful packer and handy traveller?

Has she a good memory and is she tidy and methodical in her work and duties?

Has she a good temper or is she easily irritated?

Is she thoroughly discreet and not inclined to make friends all over the place, and is she really reliable?

Is her health good and has she good eyesight?

Do you know if she is engaged to be married?

The last question must have been something of a bombshell. It is sad to think of a paragon getting over all those tricky fences, only to be downed within sight of the winning-post by the last of all.

Perhaps even employers had an inkling that they were asking rather a lot of their lady's maids, for an amusing list of 'essentials for a lady's maid' was given to the daughter of Coke of Norfolk in 1822, when she was about to get married:

She *must not* have a will of her own in *anything*, & be always good-humoured & approve of everything her mistress likes. She *must not* have a gt appetite or be the least of a *gourmand*, or *care* when or how she dines, how often disturbed, or even if she has no dinner at all. She had better not drink anything but water.

She must *run quick* the instant she is *called*, whatever she is about. Morning, noon and night she must not mind going without *sleep* if her mistress requires her attendance. She must not require high wages nor expect any profit from the *old clothes*, but be ready to *turn* and *clean* the *dirty gowns*, not for herself, but her mistress, and then sell them for an old song as she is *bid* & be satisfied with two gowns for herself. She *must* be a *first-rate* vermin catcher.

She must be *clean* & *sweet* & very *quick*. She must have ears (strong ones), eyes & hands, but as for thinking or judging for herself or being in any way independent (if especially her mistress be a Whig of liberal *principles*) she must not think of such a thing; & let her not venture to make a complaint or difficulty of any kind. If so, she had better go at once.

She may gather as much gossip as she likes, but never *tell any*.

Implicit obedience the first essential; extraordinary disinterested-ness, united with a love of strict economy, the second. Honesty that will bear the closest inspection; unceasing activity; unimpeachable good health & extreme good humour *indispensable requisites*.

She must, in short, do everything, gain nothing except the few pounds she gets from her wages & be alive to the fact that she has a very good place.

Not all employers were quite so humorous about the demands they made. In 1825 Creevey wrote about a lady with a less endearing attitude to her servants. She was, as he put it, 'very great upon maid servants. She says, manufacturers and *education* have destroyed the race. The time was when she could have respectable young women – farmers' daughters – to be either dairymaids, housemaids, or even kitchen maids, but that now she can't pick up an article worth a farthing for love or money.' There is something about her tone of voice that suggests that it was not much of either love or money that was being offered.

Employment agencies were useful in putting servants and employers in touch with each other. The Hatfield papers include a printed leaflet from Madame Lintot's Agency in Regent Street, listing over a dozen noble and eminent patrons who will vouch for her services. 'Families requiring trustworthy and experienced persons for their Establishments' are offered:

> names and addresses of English Housekeepers, Cook House-keepers, First-class French cooks, Travelling Maids, First-class Lady's Maids, Useful Maids, Trained Sick Nurses, Head Nurses, Under Nurses, Children's Maids, Schoolroom Maids, Head House-maids, Second and Third Housemaids, Parlour Maids, Cooks, Still-room Maids, Kitchen Maids, Scullery Maids, Laundry Maids, etc . . .

Employers had a wide range of specialist staff to choose from, and were asked to state what nationality, age, and religion they preferred.

In the good years, servants also had a wide choice of employment. Once a girl or boy was taken on in a great household, there were plenty of opportunities for promotion. A candle boy, hall boy or lamp man could work his way up to be third, second and eventually first foot-man; a scullery maid could become a kitchen-maid; and a third housemaid could move up to be first housemaid. When a servant was dismissed he would receive what came to be known as the 'dear John letter', giving a month's notice or a month's wages in lieu of notice. Staff who had been dishonest, unsober, disobedient or guilty of 'improper conduct' could be dismissed without any notice.

And sometimes, of course, it was the servant who gave notice to his employer. The political upheavals in France brought an army of French chefs to England, and they were sufficiently sought-after to be fastidious about the employers they worked for. Louis Eustache Ude had been Louis XVI's cook, and in England the Earl of Sefton paid him the princely salary of three hundred guineas a year. But the French master-chefs found English working conditions hard to bear. Ude complained that he had too few assistants in his kitchen, too many dishes to prepare, and with all his artistry he was regarded as no more than a domestic servant. The famous Carême resigned from his £1,000-a-year position with the Prince Regent at Carlton House because his skills, he felt, were not appreciated. Another French chef left the Duke of Wellington's service and was asked whether his master had been dissatisfied with him. *Au contraire,* the eminent man replied; if that had been the case he would have gladly stayed. But the Duke said nothing when his chef served him a dinner that would make Ude or Francatelli burst with envy; and he said nothing when he was served a dinner that had been badly dressed by the kitchen maid. He could not possibly work for such a master. Then as now there was an ocean of difference between Gallic and Anglo-Saxon attitudes to food.

In and Out of Livery

In the front-line of servants of noble households came the magnificent footmen and coachmen, resplendent in family livery. This was, of course, no more and no less than the fashionable dress that had been worn by gentlemen in the previous century. But now that their masters had taken to wearing plainer, more sober clothes, the livery servants in their powdered wigs, top hats, plush knee-breeches, braided or embroidered coats with shoulder-knots, buckles, and lace were all the more conspicuous, matching the sumptuousness of the great houses and the gleaming coachwork of the carriages. Handsome looks were an important qualification for a livery servant, and it was said that when it came to choosing a footman 'calves came before character'. The tallest footman could command the highest

'The Running Footman', an inn sign. It was hard work keeping up with the horses, so the long cane often held an invigorating mixture of eggs and white wine

wages – those who topped five foot ten inches expecting as much as ten pounds a year more than colleagues who were four inches shorter. They often stood in pairs, and they were carefully teamed as 'matching footmen' of roughly the same height and build.

Livery was functional as well as decorative, and each family had its own colours and variations which made it possible for them to pick out their own servants at a crowded function. Lord Leicester's livery was blue, the Earl of Carlisle's flunkeys wore claret-coloured coats, while at Longleat the Marquess of Bath's footmen had mustard-yellow coats, black waistcoats trimmed with silver braid, and intricate clocks on their thick silk stockings. They wore black cocked hats, pointing sideways over their ears and decorated with more silver braid and a great crested button. When they went out with the state coach, footmen carried impressive staves in their hands and stood at the back on a small raised platform. 'Running footmen' had an energetic job keeping up with the horses, and carried long canes tipped with a silver ball which often contained an invigorating mixture of eggs and white wine, to keep their strength up.

State occasions and important dinner parties called for the ritual of 'powder'. At Welbeck and at Longleat there were special footmen's powder rooms, fitted with long mirrors and wash-basins along one side. The footmen took off their jackets, hung them up, and covered their shoulders with towels. Then they ducked their heads in water, rubbed soap in their hair to make a lather, and combed it stiffly through. Powder puffs came into action as they took turns to dust each other's hair with either violet powder or (in some cases) ordinary flour. This dried to a firm paste and it was important that it should not be shaken off and seen on a livery jacket. It was quite an ordeal. Some footmen found that they caught cold from waiting with damp heads in draughty passages or at open doors. They often had to stand for a whole evening, stock still and statuesque though longing to scratch their itchy scalps.

When it came to travelling or moving to another job, livery servants needed special luggage so that their clothes would arrive immaculate at the end of the journey. A footman who went from Castle Howard to Welbeck recorded that he had two five-foot steel cases to take his suits of full- and half-livery, two leather portmanteaux for smaller liveries, and six hat-boxes. Livery usually belonged to the employer, and livery servants – footmen, coachmen, under-butlers, grooms, pages, and the young boys known as 'tigers' – were allowed two or three suits of livery each year and one or two working suits as well. Some families gave higher wages instead of livery, but it was generally agreed that servants who 'found their own liveries' were less well turned-out.

The groom of the chambers, the house steward, butler, and valet did not wear livery but had an elegance of their own in black dress coats with white ties. Servants who did not wear livery and had to 'find themselves in clothes' usually had an allowance for this, though valets were given their master's cast-offs instead. Housemaids wore print dresses for their morning work and changed into dark ones, with frilly caps and aprons, after lunch. The housekeeper wore a dignified dark dress, and carried her jangling bunch of keys as a badge of office wherever she went.

Apart from occasional shabbiness – as at Hatfield, where the un- worldly Cecils had more important things to think about – the servants must have looked splendidly in keeping with the great houses where they were employed. Creevey was accustomed to aristocratic surroundings, but on at least one occasion he was dazzled by the elegance of the footmen. 'Such cloaths,' he gasped, 'such rich laced waist-coats – such beautiful new *silk* stockings and silver buckles!'

Perhaps the last word on the subject should come from Thackeray, whose portrait of 'Jeames of Buckley Square', from *Yellowplush Papers*, shows a footman in all the glory of his livery, clattering through Mayfair to the music of his horses' hooves:

> O Evans! it vas the best of sights
> > Behind his Master's coach and pair,
> To see our Jeames in red plush tights,
> > A driving hoff from Buckley Square.
> He vel became his hagwilletts,
> > He cocked his at with *such* a hair;
> His calves and viskers *vas* such pets,
> > That hall loved Jeames of Buckley Square.

2

The Upper Ten and the Lower Five

Although there were slight variations from house to house, the domestic hierarchy was a generally accepted established system which expected certain specialist skills and services from each of its members. Those who rose to the top of the tree were very knowledgeable men and women, knowing not only their own work but also what to expect from their underlings, some of whose jobs they themselves had done on their way up. As rigidly as any trade union members today, they accepted that there was a special task for every person and a special person for every task.

The Upper Ten

The House Steward

However large or small the army of servants in a house, the house steward was always its commanding officer. He engaged all the men-servants except his master's personal valet, and it was also his job to give notice to those who did not pass muster. His responsibility for seeing that things went smoothly at all the family's houses called for an imposing presence. Lord Ernest Hamilton remembered the steward at his old home, Chesterfield House, Mayfair, as a large and impressive man who always wore a fashionable short frock-coat, and whose naturally majestic appearance was enhanced by a pointed grey 'imperial'. He tells how most of the steward's time was spent below stairs, but occasionally he came across him in a passage or stairway; he would then say, 'Good morning, Burgh', and the great man would flatten himself against the wall and reply, 'Your most obedient, my lord'.

House stewards paid bills and wages, ordered most of the supplies, and kept the household accounts, submitting them once a month for their master's approval. (This was no light matter: at Chatsworth in 1844 the steward's account came to £30,000.) They also had to be able to write a good letter, whether to a local tradesman or to one of their master's most eminent guests. As they were distinguished by not wearing livery, they did not get an allowance for clothes.

In some houses the steward was responsible for the wine cellar, though this was often the butler's job. At Hatfield the house steward was handed a list of servants' breakages, as well as claims for board wages and travelling expenses, on the last Saturday of each month. All the glasses and decanters were in his care, and a press in the steward's room contained dozens of ale and wine glasses as well as eighteen small decanters. In his office, the steward had rows of other decanters to keep an eye on – twenty-one quart-sized, twenty-four pint-sized, forty-eight large, twenty-two moulded, and five for claret, as well as wine glasses and ten wine-coolers.

A missing decanter or a chipped wine glass could not be overlooked, even when the house steward had a Whitehall reception to organize. The memo book of John Strike, Lord Salisbury's steward, switches deftly from shooting parties and tenants' balls at Hatfield, to dinners in Arlington Street, and what he calls a 'brilliant affair at the Foreign Office'. This was in 1877, and included a private supper for the Royal Family, 'fitted up and supplied by ourselves'. The evening was over by 1.30 a.m., and Strike adds that he himself 'got off by 2.30'.

The Housekeeper

The housekeeper was the steward's counterpart on the distaff side. She engaged and dismissed all the women servants except, once again, personal attendants like the lady's maid, nurse, and cook, who were chosen and managed by the mistress of the house. She ruled over the store-room, ordering and handing out supplies from there as well as from the still-room and the china closet. She also bought house linen and saw that it was kept in good trim. She kept the housekeeping accounts and submitted them once a week to her mistress, whom she helped with good works and kindnesses to needy people on the estate and in neighbouring villages. She did most of the sewing, candied and bottled fruit, made preserves and pickles, lavender-water and pot pourri, and used dark damask roses to distil rose-water.

Scones, cakes and pastries, sugar decorations, sweets, wine, and

Dinner in the servants' hall, where seating was in order of precedence. A sketch from life, 1900, by W. R. S. Stott

In the kitchen at Keele Hall, *c.* 1900

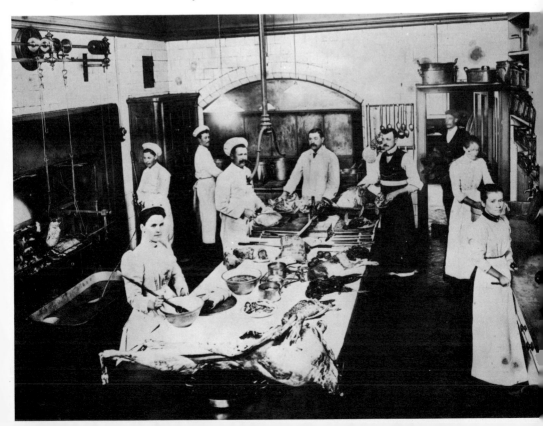

cream syllabubs and 'the higher confectionery' were made in the still-room by the housekeeper and the still-room maid. When drawing-room tea became the custom it was the housekeeper's job to make it. (It is said to have been 'invented' by the seventh Duchess of Bedford.) She also knew rudimentary first-aid, and how to make lozenges and healing lotions. Usually it was the housekeeper, with the head housemaid and a skeleton staff of a few others, who stayed in each house when the family left home, taking their personal servants along with them.

Like the house steward, the housekeeper was a dignified figure, and did not wear uniform. In houses without a steward, the Upper Ten had all their meals in the housekeeper's room, and she took on most of his duties. She was often something of a headmistress and a Mother Superior, as well as a commander-in-chief. At Chatsworth, the confectionery, pantry, plate room, and maids' room were carefully resited near the three rooms which made up the housekeeper's 'private apartments', so that they could be conveniently 'under her wing'.

Usually her day started at 7.30 a.m., when she gave out the china and table linen that would be needed for breakfast from the store in her room. Half an hour later she presided over breakfast for the upper servants in her room, and then handed out the main stores for the day. Then there was the breakfast china to wash, with the help of the still-room maid, and the round of the bedrooms to make, to see that soap, candles, writing-paper, and inkstands were all at the ready, and drawers and wardrobes in order. At one o'clock she led the way into the servants' hall, where she presided and carved one of the joints. Then came the ritual of leading her troop of upper servants back to her own room, where she once more took the head of the table and served the pudding or cheese. During the afternoon she arranged the dessert for dinner, baked cakes, and made tea for the drawing-room, again giving out the china, and washing and putting it away. Between the acts she sewed and did her accounts, with a break when she poured out the tea for the upper servants. After dinner she made tea and coffee and sent these into the dining-room, carved again at the servants' supper at 8.30 or 9 p.m., and was responsible for putting the dessert away safely.

Sometimes it must have seemed an impossible job. In 1844, Queen Victoria paid the Duke of Wellington the unwelcome compliment of inviting herself and Prince Albert to visit him at Stratfield Saye. The prospect of the visit dismayed the old soldier who had been undaunted both as commander-in-chief and as Prime Minister. Stately sitting-rooms and bedrooms would be needed for the Queen and members of her court, and walls had to be broken through so that attendants in their various rooms could answer bells when the Queen rang for them. The Duke had an awkward interview with Mrs Apostles, his resoundingly named housekeeper, when he first broached the subject to her. 'I thought that she would have burst out crying while I was talking to Her of the Honour intended and the preparations to be made', he wrote to a friend. 'She said to me, very nearly in the Words which I had used two nights before to Her Majesty, "My Lord, Your House is a very comfortable Residence for yourself, your Family and your friends; But it is not fit for the Reception of the Sovereign and her Court."' The housekeeper's room at Stratfield Saye was not large or grand enough to receive such great ladies as the Queen's dressers, and the steward's room was much too small for all the Queen's attendants as well as the Duke's servants to dine in. The housekeeper's assessment had to be accepted, and the Duke set to work to make other rooms available.

The housekeeper's day was a long one, calling for a formidable array of skills. Not surprisingly, there were a few failures. H.G. Wells, whose mother did the job at Uppark, near Petersfield, from 1880 to 1893, decided that she must have been 'the worst housekeeper that was ever thought of'. She looked all right, in her lace cap and apron, and her black silk dress, and she knew how to drive down to the Petersfield tradespeople and take a glass of sherry with them when she paid their bills. But she had no idea how to plan the work of the household, control the servants, keep accounts, or economize in any way. Worst of all, and the cause of her downfall in the end, she gossiped about her employer, and a month's notice brought her thirteen years' service to an abrupt close.

The Groom of the Chambers

The groom of the chambers was the second manservant in rank, and had the under-butler and footmen under his command. All the reception rooms were his kingdom, and he went the round of them three or four times every day to see that the silver gleamed as it should and that the writing-tables – a constant preoccupation in those days of letters and journals – were stocked with paper, quills, and ink. If any cleaning or dusting needed to be done, the groom of the chambers was not the man for the job: he sent for a footman, gave his instructions, and made sure that they were carried out.

Visitors found the groom of the chambers on duty in the front hall to announce them and to receive cards. He was also an elegant and re-assuring figure in the corridors to show new arrivals to their rooms, to open and close doors, and to explain to guests where the library, the billiard room or the chapel might be. He stood outside the door of the drawing-room or library to open or close it for guests coming down for dinner, and he helped with the waiting at meals, carrying tea and coffee into the drawing-room after dinner. Even then his day was not over, as he had to be in attendance once again when the family and their guests retired for the night, to light bedroom candles and hand them out.

At Hatfield the groom of the chambers took turns with Lord Salisbury's valet, so that one of them was always in attendance on him and Lady Salisbury. At big receptions there it was the groom of the chambers who directed everyone – visitors and their servants, bandsmen and luggage – to the various rooms. At Belvoir he was summoned every morning by the Duke of Rutland, who gave his orders for horses which would be required from the stables during the day. At Woburn the groom of the chambers had special responsibility for all meals served at the Duke of Bedford's table. In most houses he helped to carve the joint at servants' meals.

The Butler

The butler usually came to his job after a stint as footman or under-butler, and was in charge of all the footmen. He was responsible for the plate-chest and its inventory, though there was sometimes a 'silver butler' for this part of the work, and saw to it that plate in everyday use was put away at night and given out to be cleaned the next morning. He looked after the wine and the wine cellar and kept the cellar-book, entering the number of bottles given out and used each day. The wine was chosen and bought by the master of the house, who kept the keys of the cellar and gave out bottles of wine a dozen at a time. The butler bottled the wine when it had been in the cellar long enough to become clear, often getting up at four in the morning to get the job finished. He also brewed the beer for the servants to drink, usually at a slack time when the family were away from home. He decanted the wine for daily use in the dining-room, and put the decanters away after each meal. With the groom of the chambers, the butler spent his afternoons in the front hall, at the ready to announce callers. He also made the round of reception rooms, checking that blinds were drawn up or down as they should be, daily papers were cut, aired and folded – at Longleat they were ironed as well – and that the footmen had kept the fires well tended and ablaze.

But that was only part of the job. In his black dress coat and white tie he also waited at all meals, checking that the table had been properly laid and standing behind his master's chair when not actually waiting. He served cold dishes like joints and game pies from a sideboard, and after each course he rang the dining-room bell to let the kitchen staff know that it was time to start dishing up again. Then the plates were cleared away and put into a basket which had a small division for any bones or other oddments left on them. The butler took champagne round after each course, carved the joint, and brought out the salad which he had made before the meal.

At dinner, after the cheese had come and gone, glasses, plates, salt-cellars, and knives and forks were cleared from the table and crumbs carefully brushed off. If there were to be ices these were served next, followed by liqueurs. Then the dessert was offered round and set on the table. A sherry glass and a claret glass were laid at each place, and two decanters of sherry and a jug of claret were set before the master of the house. That was the moment when the butler led the other servants out of the room and it seemed that his waiting duty was over. But not so. When the ladies had left the room and the men settled down to their after-dinner stories, the master of the house rang the bell and the butler appeared again, this time with coffee on a silver salver. When at last they joined the ladies in the drawing-room the master again rang the dining-room bell for the butler and other servants to 'take away'. He then had to see that the wine was safely locked up in the cellaret (a wine-cupboard in the dining-room), the dessert taken to the still-room or the housekeeper's room, glass and plate to the pantry, and the plate that had been displayed on the sideboard to the plate-closet.

The butler had to keep late hours. At parties where guests helped themselves from an array of dishes in a supper-room, the table was not cleared until the last visitor had left the house. The butler supervised suppers of cold meat and beer for members of the band and for waiters and other menservants. There were other late-night jobs to do before at last he reached his bedroom, which was often strategically sited near the pantry, plate-safe, and plate-scullery in case a burglar might have designs on the ancestral silver.

The Valet

The valet's job, like the lady's maid's, was a very personal one. His appointment could not be left to the judgment of the house steward, as the valet went everywhere with his master, spending a great deal of time in his company, and it was essential that they should get on well. A bad relationship could, it will be remembered, lead to fisticuffs and even murder. So his job gave him a certain independence which, like his 'out of livery' clothes, marked him off from the other menservants.

Dress was his main concern. The valet saw that his master's wardrobe was in good repair, brushed his clothes and cleaned his top boots and his shooting, walking, and dress boots. He got ready and laid out clothes for dressing and changing, and packed and unpacked them when they went travelling. He would be told where they were going and what was on the social or sporting programme, and would then know without any further briefing exactly which clothes would be needed. Often he carried with him a float of £100 or so to pay for incidental expenses such as tips, meals, and stamps for the two of them.

The day's work began for the valet when he woke his master in the morning, carried up water for his bath, shaved him, and helped him to dress. Some valets made shaving soap, sometimes concocting it from a private recipe. When they were out shooting the valet loaded for his master and – unless the butler did this – he stood behind his chair at meals, waiting on him and on the lady he had taken into the dining-room. His day seldom ended before his master's, as he had to wait up till the last of the talking and smoking was over and he could help him undress and take charge of the clothes he had been wearing.

The Lady's Maid

The lady's maid was almost exactly the valet's opposite number. Her day began when she called her mistress, making sure that the

A maid dressing her lady's
hair at Hatfield House, *c.* 1820.
A sketch by Olivia de Ros, who
was often a guest at the house

Lady's maids dressing their
mistress in her crinoline, 1865

housemaid had already lit the fire in her bedroom. She then laid out her clothes for the day, carried in hot water, and helped her dress and do her hair. It was essential for a lady's hair to be brushed for at least twenty minutes every day. After that she tidied the bedroom and dressing-room, and mended, sewed, and ironed, sometimes also concocting patent cosmetics. She would have her own well-tried methods of cleaning mud from the long skirts which trailed on the ground, of removing the odd ink-stain, or wax which had dropped from a chandelier. On some days she walked out with her mistress or, if she had other engagements, with her pet dog.

A lady liked her maid to be young, partly because, like the valet, she could not expect many early nights and had to stay up till the early hours after a ball or a visit to the opera. Then a mistress needed her maid's nimble fingers to free her from the intricate fastenings of an evening dress, which was probably laced up the back. Corsets also had to be unlaced, and hair brushed and tied in curling-papers for the night. A good lady's maid could concoct soothing balsams, lotions to get rid of pimples and wrinkles, and cachous to sweeten the breath. She also had to dress her mistress's hair by tying it with short lengths of tape into little tufts, and then pinning in into puffs and curls which joined on to long wires at the side of the head.

Like the valet, the lady's maid always travelled with her employer and had to be a neat and quick packer. Often she was a foreigner, French maids being considered the most chic, while German and Swiss maids were likely to be more down-to-earth and practical. She had to be elegant at all times – not only for those evening-dress dinners in other houses, when she took her place as a guest of honour among the upper servants in the steward's or housekeeper's room there. She could not expect much free time: sometimes she would be allowed an afternoon walk on her own, and she usually had time off between eight in the evening and midnight, but there was no escaping from attendance at church twice every Sunday. A lady's maid was rewarded with her mistress's confidence and pickings from her wardrobe. Sometimes she could exact an unusual price in return for her services: when she was in Berlin, Lady William Russell had a Swiss maid who promised 'never to leave her mistress, or indeed the house, on the condition that she might keep as many cats as she pleased in the basement'.

The Cook or Chef

The cook or chef was a master craftsman who had kitchen and scullery maids to clean up for him and to prepare all the meat, vegetables, and pots and pans he needed to use. His day's work began when he came down to join the other upper servants for breakfast and perhaps presided over the teapot in the servants' hall. Then he set to work to cook breakfast for the family and their guests. During the morning he reviewed the contents of his larder and whatever vegetables in season might be available from the gardens, prepared draft luncheon and dinner menus, and wrote them out on slate or in his menu book. This was taken by him or the footman to his mistress for her to approve or alter as she saw fit. Then there was the following day's soup to make, and perhaps some jellies or puddings. After the servants' midday meal, at which he sometimes carved the joint, he dished up luncheon for the dining-room. Some cooks presided over tea for the under servants in the kitchen; and they all had a busy stint between five o'clock and dinner at nine. The day's duties were over after the evening meal had been served.

Cooks were paid more than other servants. *The Servants Practical Guide: a Handbook of Duties and Rules,* published in 1880, gives a cook's earnings (apart from his perks) as between £100 and £150 a year, which can be compared with £50 to £80 for the house steward and £40 to £50 for the groom of the chambers. Pay varied from house to house, of course. Farington mentions in his diary that at Houghton in 1813 Lord Cholmondeley paid his cook a fixed sum for each person who dined with him. Evidently this was not a good plan, as there is a further entry a little lower down the page: 'Lord Cholmondeley is noted for giving bad dinners'.

At Holkham in the middle years of the century there was a roasting cook (male) as well as a woman cook, who travelled to and from London with the family, a woman baker, and two or three kitchen-maids. Ten years later, the baker had disappeared from the staff-list, and by the 1890s all the cooking was done by one woman cook, helped by two kitchen-maids. At Petworth in 1872 the cook earned £120 a year, while the roasting cook and the confectioner got only £35 each.

Confectioners were often Italians, and seem to have been something of a luxury. One story tells of the spendthrift Duke of Buckingham, who was faced with ruin unless he cut down his expenditure. A friend suggested to him that, since he already had a French *chef* and an English roasting cook, perhaps he might do without his Italian confectioner. 'Good Gad,' the Duke retorted indignantly, 'mayn't a man have a biscuit with his glass of sherry?'

At Longleat most of the cooking was done on charcoal, and large joints were roasted on spits which turned over the open fire, since there was no gas or electricity. The cook there had plenty of fresh fish as there was a roomy fish-still, with trout and pike swimming about in it – perhaps with a partition to keep the pike from cannibalism – in the kitchen courtyard. Fish were brought from streams and lakes on the estate, and were left in clear water to get rid of the taste of mud.

The Lower Five

Some of the under servants were just unambitious men and women who were content to do a humble job. Others were young beginners, serving a useful apprenticeship before making their way up to the loftier rungs of the domestic ladder. Many a pretty young kitchen-maid nursed romantic dreams of catching the eye of the duke's son at the annual servants' ball and, like Byron's Mrs Mule, breaking the class-barrier:

> Born in the garret, in the kitchen bred,
> Promoted thence to deck her mistress' head;
> Next – for some gracious service unexpressed,
> And from its wages only to be guessed –
> Raised from the toilette to the table where
> Her wondering betters wait behind her chair.
> With eye unmoved and forehead unabashed
> She dines from off the plate she lately washed.
>
> (From *A Sketch*, 1816)

But such day-dreamers were likely to be roughly awakened by a rap on the knuckles from the housekeeper, and sent back to the realities of the scrubbing-brush.

The Footman

Footmen were in the front line of the under servants and were impressive figures. Apart from the head footman, who was sometimes known as the under-butler, they wore full-dress livery with knee-breeches, silk stockings, and powdered hair. They waited at table, both in their own establishment and elsewhere when they went on visits with their master and mistress. At meal-times, when they were not engaged in waiting, they stood behind their mistress's chair. It was their job to lay the dinner table and fold the linen napkins into elaborate shapes – mitres and water-lilies were among the favourites. When the meal began they carried each course into the dining-room on a butler's tray.

The footmen's day began at half-past six in summer and half an hour later in winter. The earliest duties were taking coals into the living rooms, cleaning boots and plate, trimming lamps, and laying breakfast. Then they carried in the meal, waited at table, and eventually cleared away. After midday they answered the front door, laid the table for luncheon, again served and waited, and washed up the glass and silver that had been used. Then they laid the table for dinner. Rougher work like bringing in coal and wood, cleaning boots and knives, and pumping or drawing water were usually done by the third footman; first and second footmen did the more refined jobs, like cleaning plate and lamps.

During the afternoon the footman on carriage duty went out while the others opened the front door and received visitors. It was usually the second footman who went with the carriage, two going only on state occasions. Carriage duty called for special skills. *The Footman's Guide*, which ran to several editions in the first half of the century, explains how a footman can keep his balance as he stands on the small platform at the back of the coach, how he should hold his cane so that it does not scratch the coachwork panels, and how to pay tolls and get the better of dishonest toll-gate keepers on the turnpike road. A footman on carriage duty had umbrellas or hot-water bottles at the ready according to the weather, wrapped a rug round his mistress's knees in winter, and when the carriage stopped he jumped down, lowered the folding steps, and helped her to the ground. 'Mounting' a lady when she went riding involved clasping both hands so that she could step on them, lifting her into the side-saddle, and then feeling discreetly under the riding-habit for the elastic loop for her foot.

Throughout the day and evening footmen looked after fires in all the living rooms. They carried in afternoon tea, cleared it, and washed and put away the china. At sundown they closed the shutters, drew the curtains and lit the lamps. They saw to it that gentlemen in the smoking-room had all they needed, and that lights – candles, candelabra, lamps, and gas – were in order. Silver candlesticks had to be cleaned and ready in winter before the evening dressing-bell rang and in summer a few hours later. At dinner they waited, cleared the table, put the plate away, and washed up glass and silver. They prepared coffee and carried it into the dining-room, and took tea and coffee to the drawing-room. When guests were leaving, footmen would be in attendance in the front hall.

As their name suggests, footmen had the duty of accompanying their masters or mistresses when they went walking, following respectfully two or three yards behind them. When they went visiting, the footman would speed up and go ahead to knock on the door so that it was opened by the time his master reached it. On Sundays a footman walked to church behind his mistress, carrying her Bible and prayer-book. In the days of sedan chairs a footman walked ahead to clear the way. When the carriage was ordered in the evening a footman always went out with it. Gentlemen visitors who came to a house without their own servant were valeted by footmen. One of their winter jobs was to collect ice from the lake, stack it in the ice-house, and trample it down to manageable size.

The third footman was usually young and had to fit in wherever he was needed. At Hatfield he was based on the servants' hall, where he took orders from the under-butler; he was also personal footman to Lord Salisbury's daughter and when he had nothing else to do he cleaned the footmen's knives. At Longleat he was nursery footman and waited on the nannies. At Holkham in the 1860s there was a 'young ladies' footman' with the special job of waiting on the daughters of the house.

The Under-butler

In most houses the under-butler seems to have taken his place among the under livery-servants, half-way between the butler and the footmen. He shared with the footmen the honour of carving the joint in the servants' hall, and it was his responsibility to see that the cook had warmed all plates and silver serving-dishes for dining-room meals by dipping them in hot water. At Longleat the under-butler, partnered by the head laundry maid, was left in charge of the servants' hall when the upper servants withdrew to Pug's Parlour, leaving their humbler colleagues to sit back in their chairs and relax. At Hatfield he came immediately under the groom of the chambers, was the autocrat of the servants' hall, and was entirely responsible for all the plate. At Holkham he was given a half-yearly allowance for plate-powder.

The Young Ladies' Maid

Young ladies' maids, like nursery maids, were, in the nature of things, temporary members of the staff, though the size and spread of Victorian families kept many of them busy in the same household for years. Their day began when they brought early cups of tea and jugs of hot water to their young mistresses, woke them, drew their curtains, and saw to it that a fire was blazing away in the grate. Then would come the decision about what clothes were to be worn that day, so that the maids could get them out, help the girls dress, and do their hair. After that bedrooms and dressing-rooms had to be put in order and clothes laid ready for walking, riding, or driving during the day.

After such outings, young ladies' maids helped their mistresses take off outdoor clothes, and between-whiles they looked after their wardrobes, doing any necessary dressmaking and millinery, and carefully washing lace and delicate linen. In the evening there were day clothes to put away and evening dresses to get out and put on. The maids then sat up till their mistresses returned to their bedrooms, where they helped them undress, attended to their hair and toilette for the night, and saw that clothes and jewels were safely put away.

The Housemaid

The monstrous regiment of housemaids had the head housemaid, who directed operations and sometimes presided at meals in the servants' hall, as their commanding officer. At Belvoir at the end of the century the head housemaid was an elderly lady in a black dress who helped the housekeeper show the house to visitors on three days each week. (The tourists of the day came from all parts of the country in great horse-drawn four-in-hand charabancs.) Housemaids were usually divided into two groups, the upper housemaids doing lighter jobs like helping to make beds in the best bedrooms, dusting, and seeing that the rooms were in good trim. They were also responsible for the

Housemaids, one in morning print uniform with her housemaid's box, and the other in her black afternoon dress with cap and apron. H. M. Brock, *c.* 1900

The page or servants' hall boy, with a device to prevent dirty hands soiling the inside of the boot. From Cassell's *Household Guide, c.* 1850

other – usually younger – maids, and checked that they were kept hard at their jobs from early morning till bedtime. The housemaids' day began at five or six o'clock, when they lit the kitchen fire, opened shutters, swept and dusted living rooms, the front staircase and hall, and polished furniture and brass there. They cleaned and blacked the grates, covering the carpet with drugget before they started, and lit fires in bedrooms and dressing-rooms. These had to be 'done' later in the morning, when beds were aired and made, and washbasins and chamber-pots emptied.

In the evening housemaids prepared the bedrooms again and turned down beds. They carried up hip-baths, hung warmed towels around them and filled them with endless jugs of hot water. One of their jobs was to keep the housemaids' closets all over the house supplied and tidied, and once a month they cleaned looking-glasses, pictures, windows, and walls. They also 'maided' visitors who stayed at the house without bringing their own maid.

Housemaids usually had their own sitting-room, where they had their tea, and woe betide any rash footman or valet found there by the housekeeper! Some were fixtures in a house, staying on with the housekeeper when the family and other servants moved away; others were mobile, like the two 'travelling housemaids' on the 1861 Chatsworth staff-list.

The Still-room Maid

The still-room maid's chief function was to work for the housekeeper, helping her look after the china that was kept in her room, laying the table for breakfast there, bringing it in, waiting, clearing it away, and washing it up. She had to be up at six to clean and sweep the housekeeper's room and to lay and light fires there and in the still-room. Trays for early morning tea in all bedrooms, as well as for afternoon tea in the drawing-room, came from the still-room, where the housekeeper or the still-room maid brewed it. In some houses she baked fresh rolls for breakfast and made desserts for other meals. She also helped with meals in the servants' hall. If ices were served with afternoon tea these were her responsibility. In most houses, bread, scones, sandwiches, and cakes were made in the still-room. China for drawing-room tea was given out by the still-room maid and she cleared, washed up, and put away everything that was used for the meal. She got ready trays for after-dinner tea and coffee, laid the supper-table in the housekeeper's room, waited on the upper servants there, and cleared everything away afterwards. One of the most famous still-room maids was little old Betsy, who had been born at Belvoir Castle, where she did the humbler washing and drying-up for seventy-five years, but never learned to read or write. Lady Diana Cooper, daughter of the eighth Duke of Rutland, whose childhood was spent at Belvoir, remembers her always laughing, living to over a hundred, and ending up with a grand funeral.

The Scullery-maid

The scullery-maids crept out of their attic bedsteads in the murky chill of five or six in the morning to clean the kitchen ranges and get them lighted. After that they set to work on preparations for the gargantuan breakfast dishes. They were little more than children – thirteen or fourteen years old – and after a late supper party they were often kept at the sink, washing-up till one in the morning. Their day was spent cleaning and scouring pots and pans, and scrubbing floors in the scullery, larders, kitchen passages, and servants' hall, where they laid the table for meals.

The Kitchen-maid

Kitchen-maids came under the head kitchen-maid and generally earned rather more than scullery-maids. They lit the kitchen fire, kept the kitchen clean, washed up dishes for the cook, and scrubbed the mighty deal tables. They also did slightly more skilled jobs like making sauces, baking bread, and preparing vegetables and other ingredients the cook needed.

The Laundry Maid

As the laundry was often outside the house, laundry maids were often considered outside servants, though they took their meals in the servants' hall and slept with the other maids in the house. They too were divided into two ranks, upper laundry maids being entrusted with fine linen used by the family while the less skilled girls did the household washing and servants' clothes.

The Dairy Maid

Dairy maids also had an ambivalent position half-way between indoor and outdoor staff. In houses where they were classed as indoor servants they did some of the kitchen-maids' work as well as their own, but their main jobs were churning butter and looking after poultry and eggs. (The cows were milked by the farm men.) They also reared chickens, ducks, and turkeys. Where there was a large dairy, the dairy maid usually lived at the home farm. Again the best portrait comes from Lady Diana Cooper, with her description of the Belvoir dairy maid, Miss Saddlebridge, 'who filled the dishes with creamy milk and churned yellow butter-pats crested with peacocks'.

The Coachman

The skill and sobriety of their coachman were of life-and-death importance to the family and their friends. When there was more than one, the head coachman drove the barouche or other open carriage, drawn by a pair of horses, while the second coachman took the reins of the one-horse brougham and did night-driving jobs like taking the family out or going to the railway station. A coachman's day began at six. The head coachman saw that the horses were properly fed, watered, cared for, and groomed, and that the carriages, harness, harness-room, and stables were cleaned and in good order. He ordered hay, corn, and straw, and was responsible for all stable accounts. The second coachman helped the groom clean carriages and harness, look after the horses, groom, and sometimes exercise them. Some coachmen were on board wages, catering for themselves in their own lodgings over the stables or in a rent-free cottage; others took their meals with the servants in the house. Theirs was a strenuous and exacting job. When the order was given to have the horses harnessed and the carriage brought to the door, the coachman might have to be dressed in livery, perched high on his box and ready for the road in not more than twenty minutes.

The Groom

The groom fed and groomed the horses, exercised them, and had the stables ready for his master to inspect by nine or ten in the morning.

Either a groom, who was mounted, or a pad-groom on foot escorted his master or mistress when they went riding. At Belvoir, the family and their friends on horseback were accompanied by an elegant old man with silver buttons on his blue livery, and with a top hat and cockade, who jogged respectfully along behind the leading saddle-horses. There, too, the head groom stood ready when the family went for their afternoon drive, holding a bunch of carrots for the Duke to offer to his carriage-horses.

Sometimes there were specialist grooms – a *manège* groom at Wilton, or the stud-groom and the keeper of the stallion at Petworth. At Longleat the fourteen stable staff included a carriage groom, a steel boy who polished the bits, stirrups, and other metal parts of the harness, and a 'tiger', a small boy in livery who sat perched on the box of the carriage, or stood on the platform at the back, with his arms folded across his chest. In more relaxed moments he used to lead the childrens' ponies when they went riding. Tigers also sometimes went out on visits with the carriage so that they could jump down to ring the door bell, leaving the coachman on the box in full command of his horses.

The Postilion

Postilions rode one of the carriage-horses and so were able to control their own pair, and perhaps the leaders as well. Their skill could be vitally important in an emergency, as it was when the Duchess of Devonshire's horses suddenly took fright at the moving shadow of a windmill. They reared and turned sharply up a bank, and there would have been a disaster if the postilion had not kept his seat and the footmen had not held the coach until some labourers came to the rescue. Sometimes there were also outriders trotting or cantering alongside a carriage. One of the best descriptions of a spirited cavalcade is Creevey's account of the aged but intrepid dowager Lady Salisbury arriving at a ball in 1829. She turned up 'in her accustomed manner, in a phaeton drawn by four long-tail Flanders mares – she driving the wheel horses, and a postilion on the leaders, with two outriders on corresponding long-tailed blacks. Her men and maid were in her chaise behind; her groom and saddle horses arrived some time after her.'

The Lamp Man and the Candle Man

Lamp men and candle men (or boys) were also important specialists, based on the lamp room with its fatty, oily, and waxy smells. The daily drill began when all the lamps were collected and their wicks checked. Some needed trimming with special scissors whose blades were fitted with a circular lip to catch any snippings and prevent them falling back into the lamp. They were filled from large tanks – with paraffin for staff and corridor lamps, and colsa oil (which gave a softer light and was less smelly) for those in the main rooms. The soot-blackened glass of the lamp-chimneys had to be cleaned, and the globes and stands rubbed over and polished. Then there were wicks to cut, and candelabra had to be scraped clean of wax drippings before they too were given a good polish.

As soon as it was dark the lamp or candle man was on the alert, turning wicks up and down, snuffing out candles, and clearing wax from extinguishers. His day was not over till the last lamp was turned down and blown out for the night. His was a key job. A careless or clumsy lamp man could make rooms murky or musty, damage fabrics and furniture with smoky fumes, and even cause a serious fire.

There were slight variations in work and status from house to house. At Petworth the lamp men wore livery. At Belvoir there were three of them, responsible for all the lighting in the castle. At Bowood there were a hundred and fifty oil lamps to keep in good trim. At Longleat the chapel was lighted by a hundred and forty candles, and every day they all had to be lit with a taper by the candle boy in time for morning service. The taper was fixed to a stick which had a snuffer at its other end, and when chapel was over the candle boy used this to snuff out all the candles. Then he broke the hardened wax off their sides and re-pointed them into shape so that they looked as if they had not been used. This was a daily drill and the candles were relit until they were down to their last two inches. Then they were allowed as perks to the candle boy, who made a few extra shillings each year by selling them to the local grocer. When he had done the candles he set to work on the lamps. Four hundred of these, of all shapes and sizes, were brought by housemaids, footmen, and other servants to the lamp room every day. They were cleaned, trimmed, and filled by the candle boy, who was helped by the hall boy, the steward's room boy, and the odd men. They did them in batches of twenty at a time, bringing in others as each lot was finished. The great lamps which hung from the ceilings on chains were too heavy to move, so they had to be groomed and filled where they were.

'And then the lighting of the lamps.' At Longleat this coincided with shutter time, a busy moment when heavy iron bars had to be fixed over the great wooden shutters. Lamps in the drawing-room and other reception rooms were lit by footmen, while the hall boy did the ones in the cellars, basement, and corridors. But that still left a great many for the candle boy, whose working day was not over till the family and their guests had retired for the night and the last lamps were at length turned down.

The lamp and candle men disappeared when gas and electricity appeared on the scene; as most great houses had their own gasworks, their place was taken by gas technicians. While there were candlesticks in every room and corridor there had been no risk of a sudden blackout, but once the candles were thrown away a gas failure could cause pandemonium. Creevey tells of one such occasion when a party was in full swing at Lambton Castle, the Earl of Durham's home, with a hazard table at one side of the hall, billiards at the other, and whist and music in the drawing-room. All of a sudden, 'lo and behold out went the *gas* from the top of the house to the bottom' and all was confusion as there was not a candle to be found anywhere. The panic was more unusual and alarming for a generation which had relied on plentiful candles than it would be in this century when, in spite of our sophisticated machinery, we have had other reasons to learn to take such emergencies in our stride.

The Odd Man

One or two odd men seem to have been employed in almost every great house, though their jobs were not always the same. It must have been their general willingness and adaptability that made them so useful, turning their hands to anything that needed to be done. Usually they brought coal and wood to the many fire-places, waited at the midday meal in the kitchen, and helped to carry dining-room food from the kitchen to the often far-distant serving-room. At Hatfield they wore livery, had luggage and cellar duties, and helped the under-butler attend on shooting luncheons. At Longleat, as well as collecting lamps and taking them to the lamp room, they rang the handbell which summoned the servants to luncheon in the servants' hall.

The Steward's Room Man

The steward's room men, boys, or footmen laid the table for meals in the steward's room and did any other jobs that were needed there. At Petworth there were two steward's room men and they wore half-livery. At Hatfield the steward's room boy also wore livery and he generally waited on the steward. He cleaned all dirty boots put out from the nursery, as well as those of the housekeeper and the lady's maids.

The Servants' Hall Boy

The servants' hall boy, or hall boy, was usually a young apprentice, learning skills which would lead him to the job of steward's room boy. He laid the tea in the servants' hall, helped with lamps and rough work, and was a below-stairs factotum.

One or Two Others

There remain one or two unusual spokes in the great wheel upon which the affairs of country houses and estates bowled along. Some families had an usher of the hall. At Petworth he wore half-livery and had the same pay as footmen but it is not clear what work he did. Confectioners, often Italian, also crop up at times. At Chatsworth there was a resident upholsterer, as there was at Belvoir, where Lady Diana Cooper remembers him sitting cross-legged 'in a tremendous confusion of curtains and covers, fringes, buttons, rags and carpets', working with 'huge curved needles like scimitars, bodkins, hunks of beeswax to strengthen thread, and hundreds of flags'. Belvoir flags always needed mending, as the winds tore at them where they were flown high up on the tower in windy, rainy or sunny weather.

She also remembers the Belvoir watermen, huge figures in great baize aprons reaching from their chins to their knees. 'On their shoulders they carried a wooden yoke from which hung two gigantic cans of water. They moved in a perpetual round', filling jugs, cans, kettles, and hip-baths. She has a splendid description of the gongman, an ancient servant with a white beard down to his waist. 'Three times a day he rang the gong – for luncheon, for dressing-time, for dinner.' Down the endless corridors of the castle he walked, 'his livery hanging a little loosely on his bent old bones, clutching his gong with one hand and with the other feebly brandishing the padded-knobbed stick with which he struck it.' He had to be heard along every passage as well as in the towers, so it seems he must have drummed away at his gong for ten minutes at a time, three times each day.

Perhaps the gongman was near the end of his tattoo, for Augustus Hare, the writer, who visited Belvoir in 1893, found trumpeters doing the job. But there was no break in the work of the watchmen, who spent the whole night pacing along passages, terraces, and battlements, calling out the hour with a reassuring 'All's well'.

At Longleat there was at one time a courier who arranged for all the family's comings and goings and travelled with them on their journeys to see that things went according to plan. In the 1850s they also had a woman chimney-sweep, which was unusual, though perhaps it was a dynastic appointment as her name was Mary Morgan and the account books for 1800–1 show that the sweep at that time was called John Morgan.

Most houses dealt with oilmen, who manufactured and supplied lamp oil, but Farington mentions a hostess who used one in the early years of the century to reinforce the skills of her kitchen staff. Whenever the Duke of York was to dine with her, Farington reports, 'she employed an Oilman in the neighbourhood to dress the dinner'. An even more unusual specialist worked in the kitchen at Charlecote Park, near Warwick, where the duties of fetching spring water, washing potatoes in it, and then cooking them were the lot of a kitchen assistant known as the potato man. It was an odd arrangement. It sounds as if some roughly cooked vegetables were dished up to the Fairfax-Lucy family in their elegant dining-room. They still owned the house and deer-park where their ancestors had claimed the questionable honour of Shakespeare's Company being among the uninvited guests who came to poach. But if, on the contrary, they enjoyed the many elaborate potato dishes which turn up in records of so many nineteenth-century meals, then the accomplished potato man must have wasted valuable time in fetching water from the spring, and using it to wash off the heavy Warwickshire loam, when he might have been reserving his energies for the more sophisticated job of preparing potatoes *à la Marquise* or *à la Parisienne*.

3

Vanished Skills

The everyday expertise that kept the great houses and their in-habitants ship-shape has long been forgotten. There was a traditional right way to do every job, handed down from generation to generation by skilled older servants to their underlings. Often this called for special rooms where the necessary equipment was based and the work was done. Most houses had a knife room, a leather room, a lamp room, a shoe room, and a brushing room, as well as the sequence of workrooms in which dirty clothes were gradually transformed into neat piles of clean ones as they proceeded from the wash-house to the drying room, mangling room, ironing room, and folding room, before the final *consummatum est* of the laundry maid's room.

Special cloths as well as tools were earmarked for each job. A list of over six hundred towels and nearly as many cloths at Harewood House in 1836 shows that there were different towels – all clearly marked – for the housekeeper, dairy maid, laundry maid, still-room maid, and kitchen-maids, as well as separate supplies of roller towels for use in the kitchen, still-room, servants' hall, maids' hall, pantry, and laundry, and by the groom, coachman, and baker. Different cloths were also ready by the dozen – china cloths for the still-room, rubbers for the kitchen, pocket cloths for the footman, glass cloths for the butler and the steward's room, lamp cloths for the pantry and the porter, dusters and china cloths for the housemaids, the laundry and the nursery, and horn cloths for the servants' hall.

Today the fuss and regimentation may seem unnecessary, but when all the work was done by hand, and furniture and fabrics were cleaned inch by inch, a slapdash servant or the wrong cleaning materials could do irreparable damage to precious heirlooms. Some (but not all) carpets were swept with damp tea-leaves while beer was used when beating others. One of the first lessons for a young housemaid was to learn how to carry her candle upright so that hot wax did not spill on the floor or the furniture. In one house there was an instruction that

The butler in his pantry, cleaning the silver. From the *Servant's Magazine*, 1868

'books may be dusted as far as a wing of a goose will go', and the maids had to remember what time the sunlight came into various rooms. At Longleat the dustpans, all numbered so that each housemaid had her own, were made with a thumb-hole so that she could brush with one hand and hold the pan and a candle with the other at the same time.

Spring-cleaning was an annual cataclysm which struck when the family was away from home. Curtains came down and carpets were taken up. Old polish was washed off furniture with vinegar, and replaced with generous coatings of beeswax and turpentine before the wood was rubbed till it was warm and gleaming again. Servants stood on long ladders to wash high ceilings with soda and water, and they cleaned the paintwork and then polished it with a cream dressing. Linen drugget was draped along the picture-rails, and slatted wooden Venetian blinds were unstrung, scrubbed on both sides, and strung up again. At Longleat, the furniture was scoured and calendered. (Scouring involved polishing metal or wood surfaces with fine sand, or rubbing cloth with soap; calendering meant pressing cloth or paper in a calender, which was fitted with rollers to smooth or glaze wrinkled stuffs.) Some of the corridors were cleaned and whitened with fine pipe-clay, and while this was being done sheets of protective drugget were spread over the carpets. Brocaded walls were dusted down with soft brushes before being rubbed over, first with tissue paper, and later with soft silk dusters. Floors were washed and then anointed with beeswax and turpentine, which was left to dry and finally rubbed over by pushing a massive lead-weighted polisher up and down over them. This was also the drill before a ball, when the floor was sprinkled with French chalk to give it a good surface.

Cleaning materials had to be carefully concocted – often from well-tried family recipes – and cautiously used. As well as melted beeswax and turpentine, which were used for polishing floors and furniture, a mixture of linseed oil, methylated spirit, turpentine, and white wax was also made for polishing wood. Blacking for grates and other ironwork was brewed from ivory black, treacle, oil, small beer, and sulphuric acid. Copper pots and pans were scoured with silver sand and vinegar; at Longleat they polished them with ale added to soft soap and silver sand. A recipe in *The Servant's Guide and Family Manual*, published in 1830, gives esoteric instructions for cleaning marble: 'Take a bullock's gall, a gill of soap lees, half a gill of turpentine and make it into a paste with pipe-clay . . . or beat pumice to an impalpable powder and mix it with verjuice.' (Verjuice was an acid liquid drawn from crab-apples or sour grapes, and was also used in medicines and cooking.)

One recipe for boot-polish included the finest champagne among its ingredients; and plate (as they called all table and household silver, as well as things made from gold and other metals) was cleaned with a mixture, freshly made as it was needed, of the best Spanish white (finely powdered chalk) and ammonia, before being polished with a leather touched with rouge (powdered ferric oxide) and finished off with a rub from a soft woollen brush. Toothpaste was made from bole armoniac, bark, camphor, and powdered myrrh, and a recipe for shaving-soap involved mixing lye – water alkalized with salts extracted from vegetable ash, which was used as a detergent for washing – with lamb suet and olive oil. Then it all had to be warmed by the heat of the sun for fifty days before the soap was ready for use.

Everyday handling of silver, knives, glass, and china followed another complicated routine. Instructions hanging in one butler's pantry insisted that each piece of plate must be washed and cleaned separately to avoid scratching. Spoons and forks must never be taken up together in the butler's hand, and knife-handles must never be put in water. Knives must be washed and all grease removed before being put in the knife-machine, as this would be ruined by a greasy knife. If several knives were held together in the butler's hand the blades would chip each other and cause jagged edges, and no knife with a jagged edge must be put in the machine. It was equally important to see that the silver was always kept apart from knives when the table was being cleared, as otherwise it would be scratched and spoilt. Glass had to be washed in a separate tub to avoid grease from silver, china, and knives. Shot was used to clean wine stains from decanters. Brass trays could be cleaned with used lemon skins, or washed with soap and water, rubbed with a mixture of citric and tartaric acid, and then lightly polished with a leather. Last but not least, each article of the breakfast and tea services had to be washed separately to avoid chips and breakages.

Before the days of stainless steel, cleaning knives was a slow and laborious daily grind, and knife-cleaning machines were among the earliest labour-saving devices to be welcomed in the great houses. But the welcome had its reservations: not the classic industrial opposition to a machine that threatened to put hungry workers out of a job, but the caution of conservative owners who were afraid that knives would be blunted as well as cleaned. The machines were large and round, with holes into which Oakley powder was shaken. Then the knives were inserted and the handle turned. Sometimes kitchen forks (never silver ones, of course) were also cleaned in the knife-machine.

Another important department where traditional expertise and up-to-date methods were both needed was that of the brew-house and cellar. Beer was always brewed on the premises and was then the cheapest drink available, except for milk. The Marchioness of Bath compiled a handbook of *Cottage Domestic Economy* in 1829, and in it she reminded local cottagers of this, and recalled that forty years earlier all labourers used to brew their own beer, whereas at the time she was writing hardly any did. Instead, they either drank tea or went to public houses for 'brewer's beer'. At Longleat, outside help was brought in to help with the beer – in 1803 William Sims was paid £5 4s for fifty-two days' brewing – and it was served from great copper jacks and leather flagons. In the dining-room, serving was all-important. When draught ale was drunk at dinner, the servant offered a 'waiter' (a salver, forerunner of the dumb-waiter), upon which a tumbler was placed, and the ale was then poured from a jug, first briskly and then slowly, to give it a fine head. Bottled ale was opened at the sideboard.

Wine was bought in bulk, kept in cavernous cellars, bottled on the premises by the butler, and decanted by him for daily use. At Harewood House, in 1805, there were over two thousand bottles of both port and sherry in stock, and a thousand each of madeira and calcavella. The cellar-book, finely printed on elegant paper, lists the wines which were in regular use: port, madeira, sherry, calcavella, mountain, brandy, rum, claret, red champagne, white champagne, burgundy, white burgundy, hock, tinto madeira, malmsey madeira, cypress (*sic*), tokey (*sic*), constantia, sercial, cane spirits, priniac, tent, teneriffe, and white brandy. It is interesting to see how many wines, which were favourites of our great-great-grandfathers, are unheard of today. Calcavella was a sweet white wine from Lisbon; mountain was another sweet wine, this time from Malaga in Andalusia, where it was made from grapes grown on the mountains; *tinto* is Spanish for red, so tinto madeira is just a red madeira wine; malmsey in this case must also have come from Madeira, though the name was also used for a strong sweet wine from Greece and Spain, and the word comes originally from the town Monemvasia, in Greece; cypress and tokey must be misspellings of cyprus and tokay; constantia is still familiar as a wine from the Cape, and was first imported from there at the beginning of the last century; sercial was a favourite madeira, made from white grapes; priniac is probably a Bordeaux wine, from the village of Prignac; and tent was a deep red Spanish wine, from *tinto*. It is surprising how few of the wines of the day came to this country from France, Germany or Italy.

Keeping the cellar-book meant entering day by day the number of bottles of each wine in stock, and how many were added and consumed. In most houses, sherry and port were the wines most often served. The Attingham cellar-book shows that in the early years of the century over three hundred bottles of each were usually in stock, and at Holkham, £58 13s 2d was paid for a butt of sherry in 1865. It was transported at up-to-date speed by the Great Eastern Railway Company, which had only recently reached the north Norfolk coast and did not get as far as Holkham till the following year.

In some houses sherry was served at dinner with every course; otherwise it was offered after the soup, and was followed by a light claret after the first entrée. When the ladies had retired to their bedrooms the gentlemen settled down to their toddy, which was made by pouring hot water on sugar in a bowl, adding whisky and then stirring it. It was a cheering night-cap for a winter evening and was served with a silver toddy-ladle.

PART TWO

Seven Houses

4

Holkham Hall

THE COKES
and their house in Norfolk

The story of Holkham Hall during the nineteenth century can hardly help being seen as the background to a portrait of an unusually gifted man. Coke of Norfolk, as Thomas William Coke came to be known, was born in 1754, and in 1776 he inherited some thirty thousand acres of what was described as 'an open barren Estate'. From then until his death in 1842, when he was the biggest landowner in the county, he was nationally and internationally famous as a successful pioneer agriculturist and a kind, respected landlord. He was also Member of Parliament for Norfolk for over half a century, the father of nine children by two marriages, and as hospitable and welcoming to his own workpeople and tenants as he was to royalty and to other visiting celebrities. After being offered a peerage seven times (under six different Prime Ministers), he was over eighty when, in 1837, he was the first commoner to be raised to the peerage by Queen Victoria, a few months after she came to the throne. Coke's father had inherited Holkham from his uncle but could not inherit the title of Earl of Leicester, because it had become extinct in 1753. Also, a second earldom of Leicester had been given to the Townshend family in 1784, so when Coke of Norfolk was raised to the peerage in 1837, he became first Earl of Leicester of Holkham.

Coke's pioneer work in agriculture has been described elsewhere. From 1778 until he died, the Holkham farm was a model of progressive and productive management. Coke and his devoted steward, Francis Blaikie, were credited with doubling the productivity of Norfolk in their time, and with bringing Coke's land and that of his tenants through the grim crisis years of the 1820s and 1830s relatively intact.

Throughout the nineteenth century Holkham was very much a family house. Coke had owned it little more than a year when his first child was born, and there followed over twenty years of happy married life before his wife died in 1800. His youngest daughter took over as mistress of the house as soon as she was grown up, but in 1822, when he was sixty-eight, her father remarried. His second wife was his eighteen-year-old goddaughter. Again it was a happy marriage and it brought him five sons and a daughter. Throughout Coke's time there,

Holkham fitted the description given of it in the year of his
second marriage, when it was said to be 'always full and very like an
Inn, for people arrive without any previous notice and seem to stay as
long as they like'.

Coke's son was also twice married and he had eighteen children. In
many ways life in the great house went on in the same genial way. The
Earl took an active part in Norfolk affairs and he was Keeper of the
Privy Seal to the Prince of Wales from 1866 until he became King in
1901. At first the family had no other houses in town or country,
though they often rented a house for the London season, and later had
their second home in Grosvenor Square. Norfolk then was remote and
rustic, but gradually the modern world found its way to Holkham. In
1847 a £6,000 steam engine was installed at 'the works' there. Already
there had been enough visitors to the house for guide-books to be
published in 1776, 1826, and 1835. Year by year more people came,
and the 1861 guide tells of great changes in the surroundings of the
house during the previous twelve years, and of 'numerous parties of
summer Excursionists' who apply at the porter's lodge to be shown
around. The railway reached nearby Wells-next-the-Sea in 1857. It got
to Holkham in 1866, when the family, their servants, and visitors
began travelling to and from Norfolk by train. In the 1860s a gas
works was built and hot water apparatus was brought to the house.
There were still plenty of state occasions – probably none more splendid than the Grand Review of the Volunteer Companies in 1861,
when Lord Leicester was Lord Lieutenant of the county and over
seventeen thousand men paraded and saluted in the park.

Unlike many great English country houses which were built bit by
bit, pushing out new wings and additional floors to enlarge an earlier
mansion, the great Palladian *palazzo* at Holkham was conceived and
constructed at one stroke (between 1734 and 1759), and it was designed to be as practical as it was magnificent. The idea was for the central
block to hold all the state rooms. These were to be on the first floor,
with staff offices in the vast cellars below so that the servants could be
within immediate reach of the family and their guests without using
the same passages. The cellars were – and are – one of the sights of
Holkham, and it has been claimed that the house has as many bricks
underground as above.

Another practical plan was to have four wings, each with a different
function, joined by corridors to the central block. The strangers' wing

Thomas William Coke, M.P. for Norfolk, inspecting some of his South-down sheep. Holkham Hall is in the background. Engraving by William Ward from a painting by Thomas Weaver, 1808

The outdoor staff, and the porter (in uniform), at Holkham, *c*. 1865. Samuel Bone, deerkeeper, is the central figure

had single bedrooms on the ground floor, with other bedrooms and dressing-rooms above. The family wing held the library as well as the Cokes' living quarters. The chapel wing had bedrooms for some of the servants upstairs, with the laundry and dairy below, and a drying-yard and courtyard alongside. The kitchen was in the remaining wing, near the servants' hall, its court and other rooms used by the staff, with bedrooms on the upper floor.

Just as the central block of the house was linked to the wings at its four corners, so the house itself was in close touch with the various departments of the estate around it. The family cash books show expenditure under different headings – mansion, buildings, servants' wages, brickyard, blacksmiths, woods, roads, gardens, game establishment, deer account, and farm. There was nothing stand-offish or reserved about the place, and there were constant comings and goings between different parts of the house, between the house and the estate, and between Holkham and other parts of the country.

An old custom which went on well into the nineteenth century was for mail coaches to call twice daily at Holkham to fetch and deliver the post. Passengers travelling in the coaches could ask for a free glass of ale from the servants, who stood ready at the door to serve them. Visitors to the house also enjoyed Coke's hospitality on what was known as the 'public day', when the park was open. On these occasions a bridge across a stream near the house would be removed so that the visitors had to keep some distance away on that side. A favourite story was told of Coke, who would come from working in the sheep-pens dressed in his shepherd's smock, and would walk unrecognized among his tenants and other visitors. One day a newcomer resented not being able to cross the stream, and gathered from this particular shepherd that his best course would be to get someone to carry him across the water. The visitor offered him sixpence to do the job and the 'shepherd', though just as old a man as his passenger, took him on his shoulder and delivered him on the further side. He also suggested that the visitor might go to the house and ask for a glass of beer at the back door. There he received his beer as well as a good meal, the return of his sixpence, and the additional information that his St Christopher had been no ordinary shepherd but was Mr Coke, the owner of Holkham.

As well as the famous sheep-shearings, the *battues,* and the audits, another regular seasonal party was the annual Christmas ball for the servants. This was held in the big audit room and the local band from Wells-next-the-Sea turned up in force, for many years headed by a village celebrity, Mr Tyzack the hairdresser. Those who thought that the days of lavish junketings- for the locals would end with Coke's death soon had reason to change their minds. Three years later, at the laying of the foundation-stone of the public monument to his memory, there were thirty thousand people in the park, refreshments abounded, and champagne was said to flow like water.

Outside and Inside Servants

A description of the Holkham servants early in the nineteenth century comes from a visitor to the house in 1807. He describes how all who went there were impressed by the magnificence of the mansion, by Coke's princely establishment, and by his liberal hospitality. There were then sixty members of staff, most of them from the village or nearby countryside. The postilions were smart, good-looking lads, often the sons of Coke's labourers. He would always try to find a suitable job for a promising local boy, who could then work his way up in the world as he grew older and more skilled. The Norfolk country-people appreciated this, and responded with affection as well as respect. Few of them needed the reminder given by Francis Blaikie, Coke's steward from 1816 to 1832, who would speak of him to the tenants as their 'indulgent and kind landlord'.

After 1814, when Elizabeth Coke came out of the school-room and acted as mistress of the house for her widowed father, Holkham hospitality was at its most splendid. Royal dukes and foreign princes were frequent visitors and Elizabeth was as efficient in ruling her servants as she was gracious as a hostess. She engaged menservants for her father and made a point of writing the 'character' or reference for all servants herself. She also carefully checked the women's dress and appearance, 'banishing curl-papers and all tendency to finery'.

Coke's fatherly kindliness towards his staff and his tenants was matched by the somewhat parental affection they had for Elizabeth in spite of her strictness. When in 1822 her father's marriage was fol-lowed by her own, Elizabeth arranged for the daughter of an old Holkham butler to go with her to her new home, and Francis Blaikie took it upon himself to check up on her future husband (who came from Yorkshire) with his own friends there. Had he ever borrowed money? Was he extravagant? Was he a fit person to be entrusted with Miss Coke's happiness? Fortunately the bridegroom passed his examination with credits in all subjects, and Blaikie celebrated the success by presenting Elizabeth with a fine topaz locket, set in diamonds, on three-and-a-half yards of gold chain. She was also left a legacy by one of her father's farmer tenants, who wanted to show his gratitude for what Coke had done for him.

The change of mistress inevitably brought different working conditions at Holkham. Elizabeth found the new set-up 'altogether quaint', the latest addition to the staff being a 'new butler who had just arrived here *in a bright chestnut wig!*' But gradually things settled down and the distinguished guests were once again received in due state.

In September 1835 the fifteen-year-old Princess Victoria came on a visit with her mother, the Duchess of Kent. They travelled in an open carriage drawn by four horses with only a couple of outriders as escort, and were alarmed by the warm welcome they received at King's Lynn on the last lap of their journey. Some over-enthusiastic navvies stopped the horses, unharnessed them from the royal carriage, and dragged it through the town and round all the main streets. Two hours later the Princess was allowed to go on her way, this time with an escort of Yeoman Cavalry.

Meanwhile at Holkham dinner was ready and the marble hall was crowded and ablaze with light. At last a carriage drew up at the door. Coke went out to meet it, a candle in each hand, and bowed low. But when he raised his eyes there was no Princess. The first carriage had brought her three dressers, who had escaped the royal welcome in King's Lynn and so had come on without delay. Eventually the Princess arrived, was delighted with her reception, and slept in the splendidly tapestried green state bedroom.

Three years later a less exalted guest was just as pleased with the kindness of his reception at Holkham. Thomas Creevey was an old man then, and stayed with Coke in January 1838, when his visit coincided with two great winter balls. 'I live mostly in my charming bedroom on the ground floor,' he wrote, 'with a door at hand to go out of the house if I like it, and another equally near for nameless purposes. A maid lights my fire at seven punctually, and my water is in my room at eight.' And he specially appreciated the attention of his maid in keeping his fire well stoked throughout the day, calling in to do this almost every hour.

Gamekeepers hunting rabbits. The one standing is carrying gin-traps, and the one kneeling is probably using ferrets to flush out the rabbits into nets across their burrows. From Grundy's *English Views*, 1857

The benevolent, hard-working Holkham *ménage* included some colourful characters. The famous *battues* called for efficient and commanding gamekeepers. None was more so than Joe Hibbert, who had been a prize-fighter in his salad days. On one occasion Coke of Norfolk had some guests in the house who knew about this and one of them challenged Joe to fight him. The others egged Joe on, promising him a good tip if he won. But the old gamekeeper knew his place. He put on his gloves, but a few seconds later pulled them off again. He explained why he had changed his mind. 'Not for twice the money,' he said, 'would I strike a gentleman!'

Another unusual Holkham gamekeeper was black-eyed Polly Fishburn, keeper of the Church Lodge and a nightly terror to local poachers. She brought many of them to justice at the Petty Sessions and was a formidable figure, with bright red cheeks, fine white teeth, and hair cut short like a man's. She was as strong as a man too, and wore a man's hat, though her other clothes were feminine. One story tells how a nearby game preserver offered Polly a shilling each for a hundred pheasants' eggs. Polly said nothing, but nodded her cropped head. Eventually she brought Coke a five-pound note and told him how she had come by it. 'There, Squire,' she said, 'is the price of a hundred of your guinea-fowl eggs.' Coke was delighted, and of course insisted on Polly keeping her well-earned fiver.

Polly was a bit of a prude. Some young men who were staying at Holkham one summer called in on her at Church Lodge and said they wanted to see the church. She set off with them and on the way one of them tried to snatch a kiss. Dinner at the house that day was at half-past three, but the church party were missing. At eight in the evening they turned up at last. Coke's lady gamekeeper was used to giving at least as good as she got, and while the boys were up in the belfry she had turned the key in the church door and locked them inside.

Out of doors, Polly could turn her hand to most jobs and was as skilled at breaking-in a horse as at gamekeeping. But attempts to employ her inside the house were disastrous. She had once been taken on in the Holkham kitchen, but the story goes that the first time she heard a shot fired outside she dropped the saucepans, jumped over the table, and was off. In 1822, after the first child of Coke's second marriage was born, a nursery maid was needed and Polly was offered the job. But the staid and dignified head nurse was horrified at the idea, so instead Polly went off to gamekeep for Coke's new son-in-law in Yorkshire. She carried a double-barrelled gun and her aim was as true as ever. As she got older she grew strange side-whiskers to match her butch style of dress – on her head an old-fashioned topper, a greatcoat with stick-up collars, a scarlet kerchief round her neck, and tough top-boots under her short rough skirt.

Another famous Holkham gamekeeper only just lived on into the nineteenth century, and died in 1804 after a long working life. Old Hawkesworth became very odd in his last years, and refused to speak to people before they spoke to him. He was a miser and hid his savings away in terror of an invasion. He would not wear the liveries Coke gave him and went around in shabby clothes with an old painted hat patched over with pieces of cloth. The locals nicknamed him 'walking obelisk' and in the end he died of under-nourishment. It was then found that he had hoarded away more than a hundred pounds' worth of unworn clothing.

Then there was Coke's gardener, Hugh Girvan. The 1861 guide-book to the house mentions that it was he who, some twenty-five years earlier, had designed and built a pretty little shell-house. A young man in his twenties, he was already in charge of the gardens in 1835, at the time of Princess Victoria's visit to Holkham. He and a children's nurse at the house had fallen in love and had married, but they kept this secret because his young wife was afraid that she would lose her job if the news reached her employers. However, the excitement and flurry of the royal visit upset her plans, and she gave birth to a premature baby while the Princess was staying at Holkham. But all was well. The Princess asked to see the baby and suggested she should be named Victoria, and in 1871 Hugh Girvan was still living in the gardener's house with his wife, two children, and a general servant to work for them.

William Jones was another well-known Holkham character in the early days of the nineteenth century. Coke had been Master of the Hounds since the 1770s and Jones was his huntsman; the vast area they hunted stretched right through Norfolk into Suffolk, Cambridgeshire and Essex, where Coke also had kennels. In their old age both Coke and Jones confirmed a remarkable story: on one occasion Coke with his own hounds had killed a fox in a London square. (Accounts differ as to whether this was Bedford, Russell, or Belgrave, but anyway it was in the heart of residential London.) Jones was famous for his skill in managing the pack and hunting this immense territory and in 1797, when Coke gave up keeping foxhounds, the huntsman was put in charge of the Holkham stables. He lived on there till 1827, when he was ninety. His whole life had been spent working for Coke, who often visited him in his last years, and the two would enjoy talking together about the great old hunting days they both remembered.

The staff inside the house were also colourful, whether they belonged to Coke's establishment or to visitors. Some of the oddest servants who came to stay were those brought to Holkham by the Duke of Sussex on his many visits. He travelled with two armed footmen, as a protection against luggage being cut from the back of the coach by highwaymen. On one visit he brought with him two German menservants, both with beards and long whiskers. They looked particularly odd because their heads were powdered, while the hair on their faces had been left its natural colour. And one of them had such long hair on his upper lip that it had to be plaited. The Duke of Sussex also brought with him two negro servants, one of whom was a very small valet-de-chambre whom he called Blackey. At all meals at Holkham Blackey stood behind the Duke's chair, looking very strange alongside an exceptionally tall *chasseur*. The first time he visited the house Blackey saw his royal master to bed and then lost his way in the dark endlessness of the servants' quarters. At last, in despair, he opened a door and got into bed with a sleeping footman who had arrived late and, like many people in those days, had never before seen any coloured people. When he awoke and found what he took to be a diminutive black devil in bed with him he screamed with terror. Blackey often lay down on the mat outside the brown state bedroom where the Duke slept, and there is another story of a terrified maid coming upon him as she groped her way by the light of a candle along the dark narrow passage between the state rooms and the inner court.

It was not always easy, far away in the Norfolk countryside, to find the right person to fill a responsible and skilled job, and a mistaken choice could prove awkward. Even before there was any idea of Polly Fishburn being engaged as nursemaid to Coke's son and heir, there had been trouble about finding a suitable person to look after the baby. A woman called Mary Humphreys was recommended to Lady Anne Coke, references were checked, there were several interviews, and eventually she was engaged for twelve months. After the last interview Mrs Humphreys asked the housekeeper what dresses she would need in her new job. She was told that she would have to be smartly dressed, mainly in white and silk, so she went home and started sewing. But it seems that Lady Anne then heard some unfavourable report about Mrs Humphreys, and sent her a message that she had decided not to give her the job after all. Would she accept three one-pound notes by way of compensation? That was by no means the end of the affair. Mrs Humphreys complained to the Holkham steward, and was sent an additional £18 – almost a whole year's wages.

She was still not satisfied. Soon afterwards a pamphlet was published in the form of a '*A letter to T. W. Coke, Esqre., M.P.,* describing the distress and misery brought upon John Humphreys and his wife and five children by the unjust treatment they have received from T.W. Coke, Esqre., and Lady Anne Coke, of Holkham, by which J. Humphreys is incarcerated in prison with his wife and children.' No explanation has survived of how losing the job could have landed the whole family behind bars. Perhaps their plight was as exaggerated as the somewhat fanciful arithmetic which calculated the damages claimed in the pamphlet. For the losses listed by Mrs Humphreys included £3 for her journeys to Holkham, £55 for clothes and other expenses, £21 for wages, £52 for board and washing for twelve months, and £30 for loss of future situations. Most imaginative of all was the final suggestion that £105 was due to her because it was 'customary, when an infant is baptized, for the sponsors and visitors to make a present to the nurse' and for her to be given 'baby-linen and other perquisites'.

Lady Anne certainly had exceptionally bad luck with her attempts to appoint a nurse for her first baby, and Mrs Humphreys must have been as optimistic as she was inventive. But it is interesting to see that such things did happen, and that a woman with a husband and five children of her own to look after could be considered for so full-time a job as nurse to a new-born baby. Or did Mrs Humphreys' lively fancy perhaps prompt her not to let on to her employer about her own large family?

Of course, Lady Anne was still very young and inexperienced. Coke's daughter Elizabeth, though just as newly-married, knew far more about housekeeping and engaging staff. One of the last appointments she made at Holkham before her wedding was that of the maid she took with her to her new home. In a letter to her husband she described her as 'a sober personage of about 30, with good health', and she was glad to say that she would always travel on the box of the barouche, leaving the two of them alone together inside. She had a clear idea of what qualities she wanted in her servants and urged her husband not to engage a terrible looking housekeeper who if she frightened *him,* would terrify *her* even more. What Lady Elizabeth wanted for this position was 'a goody sort of person, who will occasionally make up a mess of broth or sago for the poor people'.

But in the early days of her young step-mother's rule the Holkham staff did not always come up to Lady Elizabeth's standards. She had to lecture the footman for 'making himself out of breath while waiting at table and making such a wind'. Her father had complained that 'the servants snorted at him as if they had four nostrils, and blew all the powder out of his hair'. And there were worse peccadilloes than that to put up with. On one occasion a footman drank too much and fell down in a fit. Drink was an occupational hazard for butlers and footmen whenever below-stairs discipline was allowed to relax. At Holkham in the 1820s, £3,000 a year was spent on malt liquors alone for the whole establishment, including out-of-doors workpeople and household staff. With so much drink around, it is impressive how seldom the records tell of servants helping themselves to their masters' bottles.

The Holkham servants had their parts to play in the great occasions of the house as well as in its day-to-day running. In 1842, when Coke died – by then, of course, he was Earl of Leicester of Holkham – there was a remarkable demonstration of public affection at his funeral. The long procession of mourners was led by his steward, and followed by a hundred and fifty tenants on horseback. After them came a single carriage. In it sat the Earl's valet, holding the coronet on a velvet cushion.

As at other great houses, visitors to Holkham often brought their own servants with them. The house porter kept a book which recorded – with a page for each month and a line for each day – the numbers who dined in the servants' hall. As well as regular house staff and visitors' servants, there were local helpers called in for special occasions – extra waiters, for instance, and sometimes a score or so of bandsmen. At the end of the month the house porter totted up the numbers and his totals give an idea of the amount of food and drink provided for the staff. It is worth remembering that the porter's record is of people who took meals daily in the servants' hall, so in many cases each individual would have turned up for all three meals on the one day. During an average December, in 1871 for instance, when there were twenty-two permanent staff in the Holkham establishment, the porter's totals give 700 days' dining for them, and over 200 more for 'strangers'. At Christmas there would often be as many as fifty extra mouths to feed below stairs.

The second Earl was in his early twenties when he inherited Holkham and the title. He soon married, and naturally enough made various changes both inside and outside the house. There was dancing till the early hours in the audit room and in the saloon above the marble hall. Once again Coke's daughter Elizabeth looked on with a critical eye. At Christmas five years after her father's death she noticed that there was not a single manservant at morning service in the church. The following day, a Sunday, attendance was just as bad – 'as usual not an upper servant, and very few under ones'. She may well have thought that the great days of Holkham were over. But the second Earl lived on into the next century, and carried on the family tradition of public service, progressive farming, and sportsmanship. Several more chapters of the Holkham story still remained to be told.

Jobs and Wages

The census lists from 1841 to 1871, taking ten-year strides through the last century, give an interesting insight into the numbers and functions of servants at Holkham. In 1841, the first year of the national census and the year before Coke of Norfolk died, there were:

MEN	WOMEN
Living at the Hall	
4 men servants	1 housekeeper
1 office clerk	15 women servants
Living on the Estate	
1 butler to the Earl of Leicester	1 gate-keeper
1 gardener	
1 groom	
4 gamekeepers	
1 kennel man	
1 stable boy	
1 scavenger	

90

Ten years later, in 1851, with eight of the family at Holkham, the servants were:

MEN	WOMEN
Living at the Hall	
1 house steward	1 housekeeper
1 office clerk (the one	1 cook
who was there in 1841)	
1 house porter	1 lady's maid
1 footman	3 kitchen-maids
1 steward's room lad	5 housemaids
1 roasting cook	4 laundry maids
1 plate burnisher	1 baker
	2 charwomen
	1 dairy maid
	1 nurse
	1 governess
	3 nursery maids
Living at the Stables	
1 postilion	
3 helpers in stables	

The plate burnisher's job was an unusual one. He was needed because the casements and window-sashes of the house were gilded, and gleamed majestically against the severe dullness of the local brick. But the salt sea air tarnished the gold, so a burnisher was engaged to live on the premises and keep the gilding bright. He was given a regular allowance for plate powder and for burnishing tools.

By 1861 there were ten in the family at Holkham and thirty-nine members of staff. The yearly wages paid at about that time have been added where these are known.

MEN	*Wages in 1865*	WOMEN	*Wages in 1865*
1 valet	£60	1 housekeeper	
1 footman		1 lady's maid	
1 under-butler		1 young ladies' maid	£18

MEN	Wages in 1865	WOMEN	Wages in 1865
1 young ladies' footman		1 cook	£50
1 steward's room boy	£10	1 still-room maid	
1 house porter		7 housemaids	£18 each
1 roasting cook		4 laundry maids	
1 plate burnisher	£30	2 kitchen-maids	
1 postilion		1 scullery maid	£12
3 helpers in stables		1 baker	
2 coachmen	£40	1 dairy maid	
1 clerk of works		1 nurse	
		1 governess	
		1 nursery maid	

The Holkham cash books bring these figures to life by adding some personal touches. For instance, in 1865, the roasting cook had a woman to help regularly with the washing-up; his must have been a greasy job, as he was given special jackets and caps to work in. The still-room maid was also allowed help with the washing. The cook, her kitchen maids, and scullery maid went up to London in April, and were paid twenty-six shillings each for their travelling expenses. By 1865 there were two schoolroom maids, a French governess (£105 a year) and a German one (£80). The gardener received £90 a year, the deerkeeper (Samuel Bone, the central figure on page 80) was paid £80, and there were five gamekeepers (one at £80, three at £60, and one at £55). The forester received £150, and a small but well-earned allowance of one guinea a year went to the mole-catcher. The total cost of wages for all the household servants was £420 a year.

Ten years later, in 1871, the staff-list is much the same:

MEN	Yearly wage	WOMEN	Yearly wage
At the Hall			
1 valet	£60	1 housekeeper	£40
1 house porter	£30	1 cook	£60

HOLKHAM HALL

MEN	Yearly wage	WOMEN	Yearly wage
1 under-butler	£100	2 lady's maids	£22, £20
2 footmen	£32	2 kitchen maids	£18, £10
1 steward's room boy	£18	1 scullery maid	£12
1 roasting cook		7 housemaids	£20, £18, £16, £14, three at £12
1 porter's assistant		4 laundry maids	£22, £16, two at £10
		2 still-room maids	£16, £12
		1 nurse	£36
		1 nursemaid	£29

Outside
2 coachmen   £40, £20
4 helpers in stables
1 gamekeeper
1 gardener (in his own house)
1 vermin killer

The Holkham wage books show that, apart from a few additions, the staff-lists remained roughly the same till the end of the century.

In 1883, for instance, the Reverend Alex Napier was on Lord Leicester's pay-roll as his librarian. His salary of £100 a year is well above all the indoor and outdoor servants, but is less than the French governess's £105, the forester's £140, the clerk of works' £200, and the all-important agent's £500 a year. By that time Samuel Bone could no longer earn his annual £80 as deerkeeper, but was glad to accept £60 as park keeper. There were then five gamekeepers, one earning £70 and the others £60 each year.

Eleven years later, at the beginning of 1894, the staff were:

MEN	Annual wages	WOMEN	Annual wages
1 valet	£70	1 housekeeper	£65
1 house porter		1 cook	£40

MEN	Annual wages	WOMEN	Annual wages
1 under-butler	£40	2 still-room maids	£22, £14
1 first footman	£38	2 kitchen-maids	£24, £16
1 second footman	£37	6 housemaids	£22, £22, £18
1 steward's room			£16, £16, £12
boy	£16	4 laundry maids	£24, £18, £18,
1 coachman	£30		£12
		1 nurse	£40
		1 nursemaid	£14

Staff were usually paid quarterly, though sometimes there were odd weeks and days to settle. Payment was made by Lord Leicester's agent and was duly signed for – with a mark instead of a signature from the occasional scullery maid who could not write.

Sheep-shearings, Shoots and Audits

The three special occasions each year when the Cokes kept open house on a princely scale were the June or July sheep-shearings, the winter shooting season from October to December or January, and the twice-yearly winter and summer audits.

The Holkham 'clippings', as the sheep-shearings were called, had their hey-day during the first twenty years of the century. They lasted for three or four days and brought together local farmers, agriculturists, scientists, ambassadors, other foreign observers, and royalty, doing the work of today's county agricultural shows in making known new farming methods, crops and implements. Each afternoon the whole company lunched with Coke. At the 1802 sheep-shearing two hundred guests 'dined on plate' and the dinner was considered even better than the one at Woburn because of Holkham's nearness to the sea 'which gives plenty of fish'. In 1804 Coke invited all the agriculturists and breeders at the Woburn sheep-shearing to come the following week to Holkham, when not only the house, but every inn and farmhouse in the neighbourhood, was filled with visitors.

Each year more people turned up at the clippings. There were two hundred in 1810, and three times as many eight years later. In 1819 the Duke of Sussex, George III's seventh son, who seldom missed the occasion, was among the five hundred or more guests dining in the state apartments at an early meal which was followed by a late supper for house guests. The Duke was there again in 1820 and in 1821, a year of great agricultural distress, when even Coke had to take care of his pennies and the forty-third and last sheep-shearing took place. Never had so many people turned up. There were about eighty staying in the house, and the first day's activities began when the house party came out to join the huge crowd waiting outside – tenants and local farmers, Norfolk friends with their own house parties, visitors from other counties, and scientists from even further afield. On each of the four days between five and seven hundred people rode out to inspect the various farms, crops, herds, and farm processes, and then came back to Holkham at three o'clock for dinner. Two long tables were laid in the statue gallery for the guests of honour, and the others sat down to their meal in adjoining rooms. Dinner was followed by toasts and speeches; on the third day these lasted for seven hours. It seems that Coke had as little idea that this was to be the last of the clippings as that the following year would see his own remarriage. When at last his guests moved off he invited them to come again the following year and to bring a friend next time, so that an old dream of his could come true and his house would be filled from end to end.

After this lavish hospitality to hundreds of guests during the four days of the clippings came the shooting season, when Coke kept open house for three months for his friends. The Prince of Wales (later Prince Regent and George IV), Prince Leopold of Saxe-Coburg (afterwards King of the Belgians), and the Duke of Gloucester (George III's brother) were among those who liked to come each year to the *battues*. These began in the first week of October and went on twice a week for the rest of the season. In the early years as many as fifty to eighty people would stay for weeks on end at Holkham.

The slaughter of wildlife was on a scale to match Coke's hospitality. In one season Coke and his friends shot twelve thousand rabbits, three thousand hares, and huge numbers of pheasants and partridges. On one single day in November 1822, eight hundred and sixty head of game were shot and – for good measure – three people were also hit. After Coke's time the shoots went on, though less sporting methods crept in. In the winter of 1847 Coke's daughter Elizabeth paid a visit to her old home and wrote to her husband that there had been no shooting that day because of the rain; but 'tomorrow they are to kill 500 pheasants and 500 hares, which are all to be driven to one spot – a regular massacre. How different to old days!'

The third of the great seasonal occasions at Holkham were the audits when accounts were officially examined and checked. These took place each January and July and lasted two days. Joseph Farington describes Coke's hospitality in the first years of the century, when some fifty of his tenants dined at the house each day 'in the true farming style; – *pewter* dishes & *plates*; – Norfolk dumplings &c. &c.' And he added that on these days Coke arranged for all the farmers' horses to be looked after in the Holkham stables, an attention he did not give on other occasions to his noblemen and gentlemen visitors, whose horses were sent to the village inn. Twenty years later the farmers were still being entertained in the same old style. On one of her return visits to Holkham, Coke's daughter Elizabeth was happy to see the audit dinner laid ready in the kitchen on forty great dishes, with vegetables, mince pies, and twenty-five bowls of punch.

Below Stairs Dos and Don'ts

In one of the service passages at Holkham there is a printed list of *Rules and Regulations to be observed by the Porter, the Establishment and Visitors' Servants,* which fills in some of the gaps in the story of the varied company of men and women who lived and worked at the great house.

> The Porter is always to be in livery, and never to be called away to discharge other duties than those which strictly belong to his office.
>
> Outer doors are to be kept constantly fastened, and their bells to be answered by the Porter only, except when he is otherwise indispensably engaged, when the Assistant by his authority will take his place.
>
> Every servant is expected to be punctually in his/her place at the time of meals.
>
> Breakfast: 8 a.m. Dinner 12.45 p.m. Tea 5 p.m. Supper 9 p.m.
>
> No Servant is to take any knives or forks or other article, nor on any account to remove any provisions, nor ale or beer out of the Hall.
>
> No Gambling of any description, nor Oaths, nor abusive language are on any account to be allowed.

NOTICE.

SUMMARY OF LIVERY MEN'S DUTIES, ETC., ETC.

The Groom of the Chambers and his Lordship's Valet will take turns of duty according to their own arrangement, provided that one of them be always in attendance when Lord or Lady Salisbury are in the house; the valet will wait breakfast for twelve, luncheon for ten, and dinner for twelve; Lord Hugh's valet to wait breakfast for twelve, luncheon for twelve, and dinner for fourteen. The valets of Lord Cranborne, Lord Robert, Lord Edward, and Lord Selborne, will wait in rotation (if available) as they are placed; one will always be expected to wait dinner for fourteen (Double entrees) or as they may arrange, for their own convenience, among themselves.

For higher numbers, and other meals the Steward and Groom of the Chambers will regulate accordingly.

The valet will brush and keep the Billiard Table in good order.

The **Under Butler** to have entire charge of all plate and keep it in good order. To have full power in Servants' Hall, and conduct it in a strict, civil, and punctual manner. (In the absence of the Groom of the Chambers, and His Lordship's Valet, to attend to all writing-tables that are used, or may be wanted; to brush and iron Billiard Table;) to attend on all Shooting Luncheons; to dust and arrange dining-room sideboard before breakfast, and put on what show plate, cigar or cigarette boxes required; to check all undue and rough usage of plate in any part of the house; to clean Gilt or Silver Inkstands; to clean dining-room mirrors, etc.; and to be held responsible for dinner cloth.

The **First Footman** will be her Ladyship's footman. He is to have entire charge of Breakfast plate handed over to him by the Under Butler. He, with the second footman, will take equal turns of house duty, carriage duty, and valeting. He is to be held responsible for Breakfast cloth, etc., and to clean Drawing-room and Boudoir mirrors. The off-duty man will do carriage duty, picnics, tea parties from the house, or anything similar that may be required, he also will clean the Breakfast plate. Footmen on duty to be dressed for breakfast, and to be in readiness for any call from the Groom of the Chambers.

The **Second Footman** is to have similar duties to the first, with the exception of attending to her Ladyship's requirements; he is to clean breakfast and luncheon knives, and the mirrors in his Lordship's sitting-room; he is to be held responsible for the Luncheon cloth, etc.

(The first and second footmen will assist each other in carrying up breakfast and luncheon).

The **Third Footman** will attend on Servants' Hall, and always wait at Luncheon and Dinner. When there are eighteen in the house, he will go upstairs and another man take his place in the Hall. When upstairs he will take equal turns of house duty (except carriage work) with the first and second footmen; he will be Lady Gwendolen's footman. He will clean the boots of all lady visitors without personal attendants. He will take his orders in everything pertaining to the Servants' Hall, from the Under Butler, and when exempt from Hall duties will clean the footmen's knives.

Footmen off duty must be dressed three-quarters of an hour before dinner, and take the place of the man on duty while he dresses. For 14 to dinner (Double Entrees); when others than family are present show plate will be placed on side-board, and white waistcoats worn. For nine or under he will be exempt from waiting dinner, but will have to relieve the man on duty to dress.

The **Steward's Room Boy** is to attend to the Steward's Room, and be in readiness for anything the Steward may require; he is to clean Nursery, Housekeeper's and Ladies' Maids' boots; to attend to all dining-room minerals, to ice all wines; to take dinner to his Lordship's private secretary at his office, when ordered; to serve refreshment to his Lordship's messengers; and to wait dinner when required.

The **Odd Man** will attend to all Nursery meals, and to luggage on its arrival or departure from the House. He will have entire charge of the Beer Cellar, and will be held responsible that proper supplies are given out in the different departments, and exercise due care that no extravagance is indulged in throughout the house. He will assist in unpacking wines, etc., and return all empty cases. He will take orders from the Under Butler respecting the supply of Beer for the Servants' Hall, and will attend in turn with the Under Butler at Shooting luncheons.

Afternoon Duties to be taken in turns. Two men must be always on duty when the family are at home; one plain clothes man (if possible); or two livery men. When visitors are in the house, or when they are arriving or departing, the Footmen must be in attendance as the Steward or Groom of the Chambers may direct. In future valeting must be no excuse for the non-performance of footmen's daily work, it must be done in the early morning, or at off times. If it be necessary that a footman absent himself while in the midst of his work, to wait upon a lady or gentleman, he must, at all times, apprise the Groom of the Chambers, who will act accordingly.

The footman who valets a gentleman visiting the house must also attend to the requirements of his wife if with him. All bedroom hand Candlesticks in gentlemen's rooms are to be brought by the valets who call the gentlemen, to the Under Butler's pantry; and it is particularly requested that they be taken direct, and not left about in passages, etc.; this rule applies to all plate; Bedroom trays to be cleared at first opportunity and taken to their respective places, Every man in connection with the house must obey all orders given by the Groom of the Chambers, or anyone who may from time to time be acting for him.

Footman on duty the night previous must in the early morning (not later than 8 a.m.) clear away Smoking Room tray, etc.; and all Bedroom candle-sticks left in the Public Rooms and Galleries.

Cups served with Tea, or Coffee, in the Drawing-Room after Lunch and Dinner must be collected by the footman 10 minutes after it has been served.

The Steward's Room boy, and Odd Man to pay special attention to orders given by the Steward, Groom of Chambers, or Valet relating to any business of Lord and Lady Salisbury, or any of the family.

Bells must be answered at once, and Telegrams despatched immediately and delivered on arrival.

Table Linen must not be used for any other purpose than that for which it is intended; soiled linen to be taken regularly to the Housekeeper's room each morning.

Breakages, a list of, from each one to be handed in at the Steward's Office on the last Saturday of each month, with account for Board Wages, travelling expenses, etc.

General Stores will be given out at 10.30 a.m. on Fridays.

The above Rules are at any time subject to alteration to suit convenience.

For the Prevention of Fire it is particularly requested that every person be most careful with matches, candles, etc.

HATFIELD HOUSE,
October, 1896.

Hatfield House, like Holkham, had 'rules and regulations' too. This 'Notice' comes from the Hatfield *Household Regulations* of 1896

No Servant is to receive any Visitor, Friend or Relative into the house except by a written order from the Housekeeper, which must be dated, and will be preserved by the Porter and shown with his monthly accounts; nor to introduce any person into the Servants' Hall, without the consent of the Porter.

No Tradesmen, nor any other persons having business in the house, are to be admitted except between the hours of 9 a.m. and 3 p.m. and in all cases the Porter must be satisfied that the persons he admits have business there.

The Hall door is to be finally closed at Half-past Ten o'clock every night, after which time no person will be admitted into the house except those on special leave.

The Servants' Hall is to be cleared and closed, except when Visitors with their Servants are staying in the house, at Half-past Ten o'clock.

All Washerwomen and Needlewomen employed by the Servants are to receive and deliver their parcels through the hands of the Porter and on no account to be allowed to go to the different apartments of the Servants.

No credit upon any consideration to be given to any person residing in the house or otherwise for Stamps, Postal Orders etc.

From 1st April to 31st October, all Female Servants will be allowed out until 9.30 p.m.

Today these *Rules and Regulations* may sound intolerably strict. But they were necessary in a house which was full of treasures. The Greek and Roman sculptures, illuminated manuscripts and rare books, splendid furniture, tapestries, and pictures by Rubens, Raphael, Claude, Poussin, Gainsborough, Kneller, and van Dyck were too well-known, and too precious, to risk damage or theft by casual visitors or unregimented servants. And there was another reason for keeping a careful check on staff contacts with the outside world. Housemaids and scullery maids were often no older than sixteen when they started 'in service'. Coke's daughter Elizabeth was sincere in her concern for their well-being. For her it was not just a question of forbidding maids the frivolity of curl-papers and 'all tendency to finery', and of lamenting that so few of the staff turned up at church. Employers as conscientious and paternalistic as the Cokes considered themselves responsible for the morals as well as the health of their servants. Gambling, swearing, and being out in the park or the village after dark were all dangers, so they were all forbidden.

5

Hatfield House

THE CECILS
and their house in Hertfordshire

When the nineteenth century began, the Cecil family and their handsome Jacobean *palazzo* at Hatfield had been at the heart of English public life for nearly two hundred years. The third Marquess became a Member of Parliament in 1853 and succeeded his father in 1868. He was Secretary for India and Foreign Secretary before being three times Prime Minister in the years between 1885 and his retirement in 1902, a year before he died.

The Cecils had other homes, in Lancashire and Wiltshire as well as a town house in London and the Châlet Cecil near Dieppe. Lord Salisbury also owned the island of Rum in the Inner Hebrides, and from there his own ship would carry back sheep and wool. Quite apart from these, the running of the house and 530-acre park at Hatfield called for administration on a scale approaching that of a local council or government office today. During the nineteenth century Hatfield House had its own gas and water works; in 1882 electricity was installed, and these services supplied the town as well as the house and estate. Bricks and tiles were made in the brickyard, and the saw mills devoured hundreds of fine trees from the park and woods. The dairy, farm, slaughterhouse, and brewhouse all sent regular supplies to the house.

Then there was the stable, with carriage horses and saddle horses, harness rooms and saddle rooms, granary and lumber rooms, and its own surgery and hospital. Nearby were the coach-house and carriages, and there were useful lofts over both stable and coach-house. Also outside the great house were the clerk of works' office and pay office, the carpenter's shop, laundry, coal yard, lime kiln and lime house yard, and the charcoal and nailroom stores. There were various specialist workshops – the paint shop, smith's shop, and whitesmith's shop. There were the lock-up room, the oil mills, and a department colourfully known as 'corn-seeds and bones'. The pleasure grounds included the gardener's office, vineyard gardens, a melon ground, a tennis court, and a maze.

The vast house had more than thirty visitors' bedrooms, many with their own dressing-rooms alongside. By the end of the century, guests'

The stables at Hatfield House at the time of Queen Victoria's visit in 1846 were in the mediaeval palace (now restored as the Old Palace). From the *Illustrated London News*

rooms all had bells which rang in the quarters where their servants were lodged. The most splendid visitors' rooms – and it does not matter that these words mean both the most splendid of the rooms used by visitors and the rooms used by the most splendid visitors – were on the first floor, on a level with the long gallery, the library, the gallery over the marble hall, the winter dining-room, and the billiard room. Lord and Lady Salisbury's bedrooms and sitting-rooms were on the ground floor, near the magnificent state and reception rooms, the summer drawing- and dining-rooms, the armoury, the chapel, several other bedrooms and dressing-rooms, and the steward's room and office. On the upper floors were more bedrooms, the schoolroom, rooms for the children of the family and their nursemaid, and a kitchen and scullery for the nursery. There too the housekeeper had her bedroom, her closet, and two store-rooms. The cook, confectioner, valet, groom of the chambers, steward, governess, chaplain, maids, and lady's maids slept up there too, and the lady's maids had their own sitting-room.

As usual, the basement was the working headquarters of the house. The great kitchen with its four hefty elm-topped tables – one of them over fifteen feet long, and another a nine-footer – needed all the light that reached it from windows high up along one wall. Nearby were the cook's sitting-room, the scullery, pastry house, larder, store-room, china room, and bread room. There were also a fruit room, brush room, lamp room, and lumber room. In the basement too was a sitting-room for the housemaids, and the big servants' hall where the staff sat down to meals on wooden forms drawn up to a twenty-two-foot table. The housekeeper's room was within easy reach of her store-room, still-room, and lumber room. Down in the basement were also a box-room, a bathroom, the coal house, and cellars for coal, coke, wine, ale, and small beer. A passage linked the basement with the conservatory.

Hospitality for High and Low

Even in the early days of the century the Cecils were hospitable on a grand scale, and the park was open to local townspeople. After matins in the parish church came the august moment when the Hatfield butler announced that her ladyship's band would play on the terrace at Hatfield House during the afternoon. On other occasions, royal and distinguished guests were entertained at magnificent balls and house

Preparations for the tenants' ball at Cotehele, Cornwall. By Nicholas Condy,
c. 1840

parties. Hatfield is only some twenty miles from London, so guests who were not staying the night could drive back to town in their coaches after a party. Mrs Arbuthnot, the Duke of Wellington's friend, noted in her journal in the summer of 1829 that she had been to Hatfield to a grand dinner given to about a hundred people by Lord Salisbury. After the meal a play was acted in the long gallery by amateurs. Then came a splendid supper in the great hall, and they had not arrived back in London until three in the morning. Twenty years later the wife of the second Marquess was another friend and correspondent of the Duke of Wellington, who wrote to her that he was delighted to hear that a Hatfield ball in the depth of winter had been a great success. In his day the Duke had travelled as many miles as anyone for the pleasures of social life at great houses. But he was an old man now. 'It is astonishing the distance people will go,' he wrote, 'to a Ball in Winter; more particularly to one given in such a house as Hatfield.'

Hospitality there was an all-the-year-round affair. It started with a children's party at the beginning of January, followed by a county ball a week or so later, a tenants' ball after that, and then a ball for the servants. In the winter there were shooting parties. John Strike, the house steward, was a methodical man and his memoranda book gives details of one of these, for twelve gentlemen and seventy beaters, in January 1878. Dinner for thirty-five was provided at 7.30 p.m. and the refreshment room was open from nine o'clock. There was dancing to a band in the dining-room, with a second band playing in the gallery until four in the morning, when the house guests sat down to a hot supper of cutlets and pheasants.

When Lord Cranborne came of age in October 1882, dinner was served to more than three hundred and fifty guests. The first course was a hundred quarts of julienne soup, followed by six dishes of turbot with lobster sauce, and another six of cod with oyster sauce. Then came fifty pheasants, sixty partridges, thirty chickens, ten hares, twelve tongues, eight turkeys, and eight dishes each of venison, roast beef, and rounds of beef, not to mention potatoes, vegetables, thirty plum puddings, thirty jellies and pastries, cheeses, cakes, fruit, and nuts.

Entertaining on that scale called for well-planned advance fieldwork. Mincemeat, for example, was made in November to be ready for Christmas. In 1877, ingredients listed were:

28 lbs each of raisins, currants and moist sugar

12 lbs mixed peel

18 lemons

1 lb mixed spice, and a good many apples

4 bottles each of brandy and sherry

2 bottles of rum

Occasionally things went wrong. At one Hatfield ball there were plenty of jellies and ices but more substantial dishes were in noticeably short supply. Lady Salisbury was indignant. She sent for the head servants and ordered them to keep on cooking for the rest of the night. So the servants learned their lesson and the guests were fed.

By the 1880s, there were various modern comforts at Hatfield. The third Marquess was an enthusiastic amateur scientist and his experiments with electricity and telephones caused many a fire as well as sudden eclipses and blackouts. The family were accustomed to throwing cushions at ancient panelling and floorboards when they started to smoulder. By 1883 the experiments were over and Hatfield was one of the first private houses in the country to use both electric light and the telephone, and by the end of the century there were twelve bathrooms. But in spite of these comforts and the splendour of his ceremonial entertaining, the Prime Minister allowed no wastefulness or unnecessary extravagance, and he checked the household accounts himself. The Hatfield gardeners grew pineapples, and on one occasion Lord Salisbury decided that too many of these were being ripened and brought to the dining-room, so he gave orders that no more should be grown. And his orders had to be obeyed. Some time after that, Lord Salisbury came across a fine crop of pineapples in one of the conservatories, so he went straight in, pulled them up by their roots, and threw the lot away.

In the 1890s, the Cecils were usually at Hatfield at week-ends, when fourteen or so would sit down to dinner in the marble hall. It was a long, slow meal with six or seven courses, and with lavish dishes of dessert which included home-grown grapes all the year round. The courses were served ceremoniously by a full complement of menservants, but the family had simple tastes and most of them were not interested in food or wine. Servants' liveries were far from smart, and both crockery and table linen were plain, if not actually shabby.

At Christmas there was always a large house party, followed early in the New Year by another – with a ball – to which royal and other guests were invited. Most men visitors brought their own valet, and all the women had their own maid to wait on them. Before Christmas the gardeners descended on the house with cart-loads of holly and other evergreens. There would be a towering Christmas tree in the armoury, and a long trestle table was piled with presents for the servants, other employees, cottagers, and their children. Lady Salisbury distributed the presents personally, with a word or two for everyone, on Christmas Eve. Next day there was church in the morning, followed by an early luncheon for the family so that the servants could be free for their dinner. The children's nurses went to the housekeeper's room for this and the nursery maids went to the servants' hall, while the children of the family were looked after – an unusual treat for them – by their mothers, aunts, and cousins. The other great occasion when the social order was reversed was the annual rent-dinner, when the tenants were entertained at the house. The great 'tenantry dinner service' – two hundred and seventy-six meat dishes, forty-eight pie dishes and salts, three dozen butter boats, and five hundred plates – was brought from its storage place in the china room, and the tenants enjoyed a lavish meal and a speech from their landlord.

Hatfield's nearness to London involved constant toing and froing of family and staff between the town house and the country. John Strike's memo book describes a busy month during the summer of 1879. On 27 June they went from London to Hatfield to get ready to entertain Princess Beatrice, the Queen's youngest daughter, to luncheon in the marble hall the following day. Two days later they went back to town for a dinner there in honour of the Grand Duke of Baden. Eleven days afterwards, from 12 to 14 July, they were at Hatfield to celebrate the birthdays of two of Lord Salisbury's children. Then they had three days in town before going down to the country again to prepare for a big party on Saturday and Sunday, 19 and 20 July. The Prince and Princess of Wales arrived by train on the Saturday afternoon and other guests were the Crown Prince of Sweden, the Grand Duke of Baden, and the Duke and Duchess of Teck. John Strike was responsible for providing breakfast, luncheon and dinner for forty-two on the Sunday, when there was also a garden party for a hundred guests. A band played throughout the afternoon and refreshments were served on six round tables and a long buffet in the armoury. Another band played in the gallery during dinner, when fifty-two people sat down to eat in the marble hall. The Prince and

Princess of Wales left for London by a late train, and on the Monday the family followed the royals back to town where dinner had to be ready for them that evening.

A hundred years ago, when electricity was still a novelty and a marvel, Hatfield at night must have sparkled in the surrounding darkness of the park like a mighty ocean liner at sea. Augustus Hare arrived there after sunset in the winter of 1890 and left a vivid description. 'All the windows blazed and glittered with light through the dark walls; the Golden Gallery with its hundreds of electric lamps was like a Venetian illumination. The many guests coming and going, the curiously varied names inscribed upon the bedroom doors' were all part of the magic. Augustus Hare appreciated his creature comforts, and when he was at Hatfield again four years later, again in winter, he was grateful for 'the equably warm passages and rooms of this immense house'. He tells of one foreign visitor's comment on the lavish meals and leisurely tempo of life there. Madame Ignatieff, the wife of a Russian diplomat, had been one of the guests and had said, 'Ah, I see what your life in great country houses is – eat and doddle [dawdle], doddle and eat.' It was a judgment which fitted Hatfield less than many other English houses of the time. With an owner who was in Parliament for nearly half a century, and who for years was Prime Minister and Foreign Secretary at the same time, Hatfield must have seen much hard work as well as 'doddling'. In Madame Ignatieff's day there must also have been many hours of conversation – a favourite Cecil pastime, at which they all excelled – as well as regular church-going, reading, amateur theatricals, and good works among the tenantry and villagers.

Servants – In and Out of Livery

As always in the great houses of the last century, staff numbers fluctuated according to the family's changing needs. In 1841, the recently widowed second Marquess and his two young daughters had only three menservants and four maids living in the huge house with them, though others were lodged nearby and came in daily to help. Ten years later the housekeeper had four maids, a kitchen maid and a laundry maid to work with her, while a porter and a groom also lived in the house and a footman, a cook, and maids were boarded out on the estate. By the third Marquess's time, from 1868 onwards, staff numbers had grown; the steward had a score or so of footmen under him and the housekeeper had as many maids.

Unusual masters set unusual tasks. One of these fell to the young under-coachman who was Lord Salisbury's 'tiger'. The old Prime Minister was a big man, very corpulent and heavy. By way of taking exercise he liked to tricycle along the asphalted paths in the park and he ordered the tiger to come with him to give him a helpful push where the paths sloped uphill. On the way down he would call to him to 'jump up behind' and the tiger would hop on to the back of the tricycle, with his hands on the Prime Minister's broad shoulders, and the old man and his young coachman would free-wheel merrily downhill together.

Even when the family and their visitors were not at Hatfield there was plenty to be done to keep things in running order. A daughter-in-law who first knew the house soon after her engagement in 1894 remembered 'tons of beeswax' being used on the ancient panelling. The oak panels were rubbed down with beer every autumn. 'There was at that time,' she remembered, 'a tipsy old housekeeper and I rather wondered. . .' It seems that Lady Salisbury had not made a good choice in 1890, when a new housekeeper had to be found, although a bundle of old papers still show how carefully the appointment was made. By then John Strike, the old house steward, had retired and was living at Hastings, and there is a letter from him to Lord Salisbury's private secretary, who must have written asking Strike for advice. He answered that the best plan would be for Lady Salisbury to ask her friends if they knew anyone suitable. If it came to advertising, it would be wiser not to mention Hatfield by name and to insist on applicants having experience of working in the same kind of house. Hotel work was not a suitable background since it was 'very different from the unavoidable uncertainty of a private family'. Strike recommended May's, in Piccadilly, as a good office for receiving replies.

His advice was followed and a few days later an advertisement appeared in *The Times* and *Morning Post*:

HOUSEKEEPER WANTED, *for a large country house. A person is required, of good address, who has filled a similar position. Write, stating qualifications, to S.N., May's Advertising Offices, 162 Piccadilly, W.*

There were plenty of replies. One applicant had already worked at Hatfield for three years as head still-room maid, and wrote that she thoroughly understood still-room and dairy work, charge of linen and looking after servants. But housekeepers had to be commanding figures, and this application has a note on it: 'Good but perhaps too small a woman'. Another applicant claimed to understand thoroughly 'all the duties as housekeeper, supervision of servants, linen and stores, desserts, flowers, a thorough needlewoman, catering if required'. Industriousness, early rising, membership of the Church of England, being domesticated and an abstainer were, it seems, good qualities for a would-be housekeeper to offer. At last fourteen of the applicants were short-listed and asked to come to be interviewed. Travelling expenses were paid and Lady Salisbury saw the women herself. Some of them were asked to come a second time but it was still hard to find the right person. One applicant was offered the job, but wrote that she felt obliged to decline the honour as she was not quite strong enough to manage such a large house. The papers inconclusively peter out, leaving a question mark against the memory of the tipsy old housekeeper. How could such careful sifting have given the job to her?

Two other Hatfield posts needed filling in the 1890s. Another bundle of letters and newspaper cuttings includes advertisements from footmen who wanted employment; they all mention their height and the wages required. An Austrian applied for the position of first footman at Hatfield, but he was evidently not considered as the verdict 'No Austrian' appears inexorably on his letter. Madame Elsie, of Langham Place, wrote to say that she had 'a very superior First Footman on her books', but once again the trail fades out without revealing whether he remained on the books or settled to work at Hatfield.

The papers are more explicit about the appointment of a stud groom. The job went to a man of thirty-six who weighed ten stone and had a wife and one child. Other applicants for the job enclosed references affirming their honesty, steadiness and sobriety, and they always mentioned how much they weighed. One man offered to send 'testimonials for nineteen years' service with different Noblemen'. The thirty-six-year-old stud groom must have been a promising man to get the job in the face of such strong competition.

Advertisements and applications sound chilly and impersonal, but servants who stayed for years often became close family friends. There are only three people who were not members of the family in the Cecil graveyard at Hatfield. Two were sisters who were nurse and housekeeper at the big house for thirty-six and twenty-nine years respectively; the other is Caroline Hodges, the children's nurse, whose tombstone tells that she 'lived in their house for 43 years, a loved and trusted friend'.

The duties of the livery men in 1896 are described on a printed order card which is still among the Hatfield papers. Though neither of these usually wore livery, the groom of the chambers and Lord Salisbury's valet took turns so that one or the other was always in attendance when Lord or Lady Salisbury was at the house. Lord Salisbury's valet waited at breakfast and dinner for twelve, and luncheon for ten. It was also his job to brush the billiard table and keep it in good trim. Each of Lord Salisbury's five sons had his own valet, who took his turn waiting at table. The under-butler had charge of all the plate and had 'full power' in the servants' hall, which he had to conduct 'in a strict, civil and punctual manner'. He attended at shooting luncheons, dusted and arranged the dining-room sideboard before breakfast, and put plate as well as cigar and cigarette boxes on show. He kept a look-out for any rough handling of plate, and cleaned gilt and silver inkstands and dining-room mirrors. He also stood in for the groom of the chambers and Lord Salisbury's valet when they were away, seeing that writing-tables were well supplied, and both ironing and brushing the billiard table.

The first footman was Lady Salisbury's footman. He had full responsibility for the breakfast plate which the under-butler handed over to him, and cleaned the mirrors in the drawing-room and the boudoir. He and the second footman took equal turns at house duty, carriage duty, and valeting; the second footman's duties were much the same as those of the first footman except that he did not serve as Lady Salisbury's personal footman. The third footman attended in the servants' hall and always waited at luncheon and dinner. When there were eighteen in the house he went upstairs, leaving his place in the hall to another man. He was personal footman to Lord Salisbury's daughter, and cleaned the boots of all lady visitors who came without their own attendants. He took his orders for his work in the servants' hall from the under-butler, and when he had no hall duties he cleaned the footmen's knives. When off duty, footmen had to be dressed three-quarters of an hour before dinner, and they stood in for the man on duty while he dressed. When the family had visitors, white waistcoats had to be worn by footmen, and show plate was displayed on the sideboard.

ORDER OF LIVERIES.

LIVERIES are given 1st April and 1st October of each year. Evening Liveries every Twelve Months. Tweed Jackets every Twelve Months (except the Hall Porter and Steward's Room Boy, they have a Tweed Suit). Hats, Gloves, and Stockings every Six Months, except on special occasions, such as Drawing Rooms, Weddings, etc. Orders for Gloves and Stockings for them will be issued from time to time as required. Macintoshes are given according to wear.

When Evening Liveries have been worn Six Months from date of entry into service, the wearer is entitled to a New Suit on the 1st of April prox. If within Six Months the wearer is not entitled to a New Suit until the following April. When Morning Liveries have been worn Three Months from date of entry, the wearer is entitled to a New Suit either in April or October, according to date of entry, but if not worn Three Months the wearer is not entitled to a Suit until the next term, or issue of Liveries.

Overcoats have to be worn Twelve Months before the wearer is entitled to another on the aforesaid date, 1st of April.

The same rule applies to giving up Liveries on leaving service. Within the above periods they are Lord Salisbury's property, over those periods they are the wearer's property.

Stable Liveries are given and retained on the same system.

Hatfield House,
January, 1900.

'Order of Liveries' from the Hatfield *Household Regulations* of 1900

The steward's room boy looked after things in the steward's room and did whatever the steward asked him. He cleaned boots for the nursery, the housekeeper, and the lady's maids, and had the worrying job of looking after luggage on its way to and from the house. He was responsible for the beer cellar and its contents and had to avoid extravagance throughout the house. He helped to unpack wines, returned all empty cases, and took turns with the under-butler in attending shooting luncheons.

Candles made a lot of work for the valets. When they called the gentlemen in the mornings, they collected all hand candlesticks from their bedrooms and took them to the under-butler's pantry. This had to be done promptly: no candlesticks were to be left about in passages. The footman on duty the previous night had to clear away the smoking room tray, as well as all bedroom candlesticks that had been left in the public rooms and galleries, by eight o'clock the next morning.

The livery servants must have been a handsome and colourful crew. Among the Hatfield papers a brochure from a shop in Conduit Street lists the menservants' clothes:

Coachman's suit	from £5 0 0 to £5 14 0
Footman's suit	from £4 15 0 to £5 5 0
Tweed morning suits	from £3 5 0 to £4 4 0
Melton morning suits	from £3 15 0 to £4 10 0
Box great coats	from £4 4 0 to £4 15 0
White buckskin breeches	£2 2 0
Leather breeches	£3 10 0
Drab kersey breeches	£1 10 0
Gaiters	18 shillings
Drawers	4s 6d a pair
Sleeves to waistcoat	3s 6d

The Outside Staff

The staff who worked outside the house at Hatfield are listed, with their duties and wages, in long rows of massive leather-bound *Labour Books*, one for each year. In 1886 it took twenty-two men gardeners, helped by two women and nine boys, to care for the pleasure grounds and kitchen garden. Keepers and watchers, whose work included the useful task of 'spreading mole heaps', numbered nine men and two boys. There were six men and a boy in the stables, seventeen, woodmen, and nine parkmen, with three boys to help them. The gas maker was responsible for making gas as well as for hot water in the house, and the man who was both smith and wheeler had to turn his hand to repairing a lady's phaeton, as well as to painting water-cans. There were four men in the office and one to mark the tennis court. Then there were laundrymen, bricklayers, plasterers, painters, plumbers, glaziers, sawyers, gravel and chalk diggers, and, of course, agricultural labourers for dairy and poultry work.

The *Labour Books* tell of a varied assortment of jobs that were entered as 'sundry labour'. Each of the gates through the park had someone at the ready to open and close it, chaff needed cutting, the turbine had to be cleaned out, and a foundation had to be built for a water-wheel. There were always field gates to make, fences to mend, and manure to cart. Bird-minding, hedge-trimming, ditch-digging, and draining were other every day jobs on the list. The *Labour Books* also contain notes of wages paid to staff who were ill or pensioned-off, and of work done at different times by the various teams of horses, the bullocks and the traction engine.

A clear picture of the formidable array of outside equipment, and the buildings which housed it, is given in an inventory which was made for probate valuation when the second Marquess died in 1868. The stable staff had eleven carriage horses, nine saddle horses, seven ponies, and a cob to look after. The list of carriages shows how much less versatile and adaptable these were than the cars of today. A great house like Hatfield needed a large number for the different jobs they had to do. There were two elegant town-built britzkas, 'painted blue and black, lined with blue Morocco leather', a dog-cart, a Croydon basket pony carriage, and a 'very neatly painted town-built Brougham'. Carriages drawn by a pair of horses or ponies were the omnibus, the pony phaeton, the nursery carriage, the brake, and the Irish car. There was also a luggage cart, a pony gig, a single-horse brake, two light spring carts, and three carriage setters.

Then there were two roomfuls of gleaming harness. The first of these contained two sets for the brougham, three sets each for pair horses and leading horses, and one set each of single and double brake harness and single and double pony harness. There were four postilion saddles, two false boots, six whips, and two special postilion whips. The second harness room housed a set of luggage horse harness, two horse muzzles, two dumb jockeys, a lunging rein, a harness horse, and grooming gear; there were also eight horse and dandy brushes, three water brushes, and some cleaning bathers.

Riding and side-saddles, donkey saddles with paniers, and pillar and head collar chains were kept in the saddle room, as well as head stalls, horse rollers, stable rubbers, horse rugs and hoods, holsters and bandages. The stablemen might be said to be married to their horses, taking them on for better and for worse, in sickness and in health. The surgery was equipped with a blood-letting stick, a pewter enema, a macerating plate, a balling iron, a drenching horn, a set of hobbles, and over a hundred drug bottles.

There were various well-equipped workshops for specialist craftsmen. The wheeler's stock-in-trade was a fragrant mountain of different woods in plank, as well as smoothly turned spokes, felloes (wooden wheel-rims), and naves (wooden hubs) for making new wheels and mending broken ones. The smith and the whitesmith (who worked in tin and also polished and finished metal goods) each had a pair of anvils and a block, as well as stalwart iron vices and forging tools.

The nailroom was stocked with screws, nails, hinges, bolts, wire, glue, whiting, and tar. It also had brushes, glass-paper, sash weights for windows, locks, traps, axle-tree boxes for carts and carriages, and stench traps for sewers. The brewhouse was another important department, equipped on an almost industrial scale. It had one long deal and three smaller beer shoots, three mash rules (mash is the mixture of malt and hot water which makes wort for brewing), and a stout beer-truck on wheels. There were two long lengths of leather hose, a large iron fire hoe and rake, a pair of twelve-foot beer pulleys, and a wooden beer funnel. There were also two fir working stillions (troughs to catch the yeast), a jigger pump, a six-foot oak drink-stall, and an iron-bound yeast tub. A giant 144-gallon beer vat and twenty-one thirty-six gallon casks stood ready to hold the brew.

The slaughterhouse had its sheep rack and chopping block, a bullock rope, pulley and tree, and a mighty weighing machine with its set of weights. The laundry had mangles, a rinsing tub, a clothes drainer, and clothes horses, as well as a patent wringing machine with a winch, and large wicker laundry baskets. The ironing was done with twelve flat irons on blankets spread over long tables. The dairy held a well-scrubbed array of milk cans and pails, churns, butter tins, cream pots, and a wooden butter tub. There were also the saw mills, with trees of different species by their hundreds lying unsawn or already in planks, the brickyard with its tiles and bricks by the thousand, and the carpenter's shop which was equipped with an exhaustive selection of machines for sawing, planing, morticing, grooving, moulding, and tenoning.

Kings and Queens

Even before the third Marquess was born in 1830, nineteenth-century Hatfield was the scene of some stately receptions. In 1800, George III and Queen Charlotte spent a day there and drove back to London that same evening. The Prince Regent was a frequent visitor before he came to the throne. The Duke of York enjoyed a day's shooting at Hatfield in 1826, and his sister-in-law Adelaide, wife of the future William IV (who was then Duke of Clarence), was also a guest. The Duke of Cumberland, another of George III's sons, was one of a large party who were entertained at the house in 1833.

Queen Victoria came on a state visit in 1846, before she had been ten years on the throne. In 1844 she had sent word that she would be coming, so work was put in hand to restore the rooms which had been destroyed in the disastrous fire of 1835, when the old Marchioness was burned to death. Then in 1845 the Queen announced that she would not be coming that year after all; the urgency was over, and the repairs went slowly on. But on 1 October, 1846, a message came from the Queen to say that she would be arriving in three weeks' time, and would stay from 22 to 24 October. Lord Salisbury was away in the Isle of Rum, and the news did not reach him until 12 October, when he was in Liverpool. Orders were given to prepare the house and three days of festivities at top speed, but time was so short that the coverlet was being laid on the Queen's magnificent bed as her carriages drove into the park. Never had the motto of the Cecil family – *sero sed serio*, late but in earnest – been more truly fitting to the occasion.

The rooms for the Queen and Prince Albert were not the only ones that had to be made ready. A big house party was invited and the servants whose rooms were in the north passage were moved out of them to provide beds for unmarried gentlemen visitors. Extra staff, wearing plain clothes but recognizable by silver badges on their sleeves, were called in to help the Hatfield livery servants. On the first evening the

The banquet at Hatfield House, given in honour of Queen Victoria's visit in 1846. The Queen is seated on the right. From the *Illustrated London News*

guests sat down to dinner with the band of the Hertfordshire Militia playing in the music gallery. Next day there was luncheon upstairs in the winter dining-room, and in the evening three hundred guests arrived for a splendid dinner, and went on to dance until two in the morning. Some must have been invited to the ball but not to the dinner, as there are records of six hundred people at the ball, while a hundred and thirty carriages, with their horses and coachmen, had to be looked after too. The troops of the Hertfordshire Yeomanry were in attendance and were served with dinner in the riding house. Guests stood to eat their supper at tables laid round three sides of the marble hall, but the Queen and the Prince, with a small party, sat down to their meal at a round table near the music gallery. Breakfast on Sunday was in the winter dining-room, though on both mornings the Queen and Prince Albert had theirs privately in their own rooms. They drove away in the afternoon.

Another royal visitor was the Queen of Holland, who was a close friend of the second Marchioness. She came to stay at Hatfield in 1867 and enjoyed her personal, informal visit. Like her descendants today she had homely, simple tastes. 'The ceremony of eating is certainly one of the tortures of life,' she said after a dinner in honour of the Czar which lasted from six in the evening until eleven o'clock at night. She wrote in advance that she would come to Hatfield in unregal modest style. 'Do you allow me to bring two ladies and a gentleman?' she asked in her letter. 'I could leave Madame de Pabst at Claridge's, but there is always a good deal of discontent and jealousy, and a Queen is no free agent.'

One royal visit was cut short by an attempted assassination. In June 1878, the Crown Prince and Princess of Germany were week-ending at Hatfield with a large and distinguished party which included Prince and Princess Christian of Denmark, and Lord Beaconsfield. (1878 was the year of his and Lord Salisbury's joint triumph at the Congress of Berlin.) Forty-two sat down to dinner on the Saturday evening, and all went well until the next afternoon when most of the guests had gone driving. While they were out a telegram was delivered, bringing the news that an anarchist had shot at, and wounded, the old Kaiser. The steward at once sent a boy with one of the German party to find the Crown Prince and bring him back to the house. A special train was ordered, carriages were made ready and horses harnessed, and at 6.30 p.m. the German visitors took their leave, travelling from

Hatfield to London, and from there onwards by the main train from Charing Cross.

In July 1887, forty years after her earlier visit, Queen Victoria came to Hatfield again. By then she was a great-grandmother and had been an inconsolable widow for over thirty years. This time her host was her Prime Minister and Foreign Secretary, and the visit was part of the royal jubilee celebrations. As well as his Queen, Lord Salisbury's guests included five other reigning kings and queens, and five crown princes with their princesses and retinues. The plan for the day's events is among the papers at Hatfield. At 10 a.m. the Queen's horses and carriages arrived, and at 1.25 p.m. a special train brought the bandsmen and their instruments. The Queen left Windsor station by rail at 3.35, arriving at Hatfield at 4.45. Tea was served soon after 6 p.m. in a pavilion on the east terrace, above the Hatfield maze. The Queen took her tea nearby but inside the house, in Lady Salisbury's morning room, and she left again by train at 7.10. She got back to Windsor at 8.20, ten minutes before her horses and carriages set off to follow her on their return journey.

There was an unusually exotic occasion in July 1889, when Nasr-ed-Din, Shah of Persia, came on a two-day visit. The Shah brought with him a large and colourful retinue; the Hatfield room-list, decoratively filled in in Persian script, records that the Grand Vizier retired to bed in the rose room. As a special compliment, bedrooms on two floors of the house flaunted the unaccustomed fancy dress of authentic or improvised oriental furniture. Lord Salisbury's English guests included the Prince and Princess of Wales, the Princes Albert Victor and George, and the Princesses Victoria and Maud.

Merely getting the chief visitors to and from the house called for precision planning. Special trains had been ordered from the Great Northern Railway office at King's Cross. Two broughams went off to Hatfield station to meet the train which arrived there at 2.24 p.m., bringing guests back and setting them down at the south front where they were formally received by Lady Salisbury. At 4.12 a brake went to fetch the Princes and Princesses, while a large cart brought their luggage, and horses went to the station to be ready to be harnessed to the Shah's fourgon (a baggage-carrying trailer). The next two hours saw some busy unpacking, arranging, and preparing before the large brougham drew up at the house to take Lord Salisbury to meet the Prince of Wales and his party at the station at 6.25. A four-horse landau and a barouche also went to bring the guests to the south entrance of the house, where they were received and welcomed. Half an hour later the brougham again called for Lord Salisbury, and the same carriages and horses, with three extra broughams, went to fetch the Shah and his suite.

The guests arrived on the Sunday and stayed till the next evening. On the Monday another special train brought more guests to a grand luncheon party in the marble hall, which was resplendent with palms, carnations and ferns, with bowls of roses on the tables. The head gardener had directed the decorations and every palm, flower and plant had been grown in the Hatfield conservatories and gardens. Other towering palms stood like sentries on the grand staircase; and ferns and exotics as well as palms were arrayed in the rooms used by the Shah and the royal guests, and filled the great fireplaces and window sills in the north gallery.

There was hardly a moment without music. The band of the Hertfordshire Militia played at the south front of the house where the guests were received, and the band of the Royal Engineers was heard in the north gallery during luncheon as well as in the gardens afterwards, during the reception. At the Monday garden party there were nearly two thousand guests, many of them local county people who had written to apply for tickets admitting them to the park. One dramatic mishap to a member of the Shah's retinue was reported in the Press. A man who held the resounding title of Keeper of the Shah's Diamonds was checking the luggage as it was being loaded on to the royal train. Perhaps he was over-conscientious: at all events the carriages with their exotic passengers chugged away without him. The Shah's diamonds were not accustomed to travelling without their escort, and the superintendent of police had the presence of mind to jump on the moving train as a stand-in for the missing custodian. Fortunately there was an ordinary train going the same way five minutes later so he soon caught up with his royal master and the jewels. Of course, many other guests who came to stay at Hatfield brought priceless jewellery with them, even if they managed to make do without a Keeper of the Diamonds. English titles were certainly simpler. The Shah's retainers must have been surprised to learn the homely name of the servant in elegant livery who took care of all visitors' luggage, however many sparkling tiaras and parures it might contain. At Hatfield this trusted position was held by the 'odd man'.

6

Petworth House

THE WYNDHAMS
and their house in Sussex

Petworth House, in Sussex, built in the seventeenth century, was famous for its hospitality in the nineteenth century. The third Earl of Egremont (1751–1837) was an enthusiastic and generous patron of the arts, and he welcomed many painters and sculptors at the house for a month or more at a time. Constable, Flaxman, Nollekens, and Haydon often came to stay. Turner painted some of his finest pictures at Petworth and had his own studio there. Orders were given that he was not to be disturbed when he was working, and even Lord Egremont had to give a special tap on the door before his guest would open it.

Life at Petworth was an odd mixture of grandeur and informality. The family had its own private fire brigade, which manned a horse-drawn engine carrying a giant brass boiler, and yet everyday life there was easy-going and lavish for the family, their guests and servants. In the 1830s Charles Greville noted in his diary that there were three hundred horses in the stables at Petworth and the house was 'like a great Inn, where there was nothing to pay, but where the guests were not very attentively served'. Thirty years earlier Farington said that Lord Egremont lived magnificently, and always had between ten and thirty people sitting down to dinner at six o'clock in either the square dining-room or the little dining-room facing the park. Hospitality was at its most splendid on special occasions like the June night in 1814 when the Prince Regent, the Grand Duchess of Oldenburgh, her brother the Czar of Russia, and their numerous retinue stayed at the house.

The third Earl died in 1837, the year Queen Victoria came to the throne. He did not marry the woman who was the mother of his children until many years after they were born, so the title passed to a nephew. His eldest son, George Wyndham, succeeded him as the owner of Petworth and was created first Baron Leconfield in 1859.

The Servants

The Petworth House Archives, as well as memoirs and letters of the day, have a lot to say about the servants there. Numbers varied from

The horse-drawn fire engine from Petworth House, where the family had its own private fire brigade

The laundry at Petworth, *c.* 1890, where the ironing was done. The irons heating on the boiler would have been flat irons, as well as special-purpose irons

year to year. In 1819 there were fifty-two in the house – nineteen 'upper servants' based in the steward's room, as well as twenty in the servants' hall and thirteen in the parlour. By 1831 the number had grown to ninety-seven, with a new group of eighteen to look after the nursery. Three years later there were seventy-three in the servants' hall, and the total of house servants was a hundred and thirty-five.

A letter from Thomas Creevey gives an amusing picture of Petworth servants in 1828, when he and a party of friends stayed there. The guests were treated to a first-class dinner of turtle, venison, moor game, and other dishes, and the servants who waited on them were 'very numerous, tho' most of them very advanced in years and tottered, and comical in their looks'. A son-in-law of Lord Egremont explained to Creevey that there were more servants at Petworth 'of both sexes, and in all departments, than in any house in England, that they were all very good in their way, but that they could not stand being put out of it, and were never interfered with, that they were all bred upon the spot, and all related to each other'.

In those days house servants were expected to stay up at night as long as they might be needed by the family and their guests. But at Petworth both family and servants were used to going to bed early, and when Creevey and his friends stayed there the Petworth ladies had all retired by half past ten. A footman brought a glass of wine to the chaplain, and Creevey's friend, Lord Sefton, who knew the ways of the house, said to him, 'You'd better take this opportunity of getting some too, or you'll be done.' Creevey followed his advice and asked the footman to bring him a glass, but he returned a few minutes later to say that the butler had gone to bed. This caused general amazement and Creevey 'thought Sefton would have burst at this, as being much too good a thing to have ever happened'.

However, the servants made up for it the next morning. Creevey was up at nine and went into the hall. There he found 'two gentlemen out of livery, and the foot boy with coffee pots, tea pots, kettles, chafing dishes to keep rolls etc. hot, and everthing in the eatable way'. He was asked whether he would like his breakfast at once, and where he would choose to have it. It would be served any time between nine and midday.

Annual pay-rates to servants, and the actual amounts that had been handed over, were carefully recorded in the big leather-bound wage

A page from one of the
Petworth wage books, 1838

Date	No of Days	Rate of Pay	To Men & Women working in the House	To Do in the Laundry	Stables & Paddocks	Kennels	Lodge Keepers	Under Game & Park Keepers	Pensioners	Sundries	Total
Bght up											35 10
...nes Richardson	twenty Footman	4	2 0	—	—	—	—	—	—	—	
...r Dilloway	6	2/	0 12 0	—	—	—	—	—	—	—	
...nes Streets	—	—	0 12 0	—	—	—	—	—	—	—	
...Herrington	—	1/8	0 10 0	—	—	—	—	—	—	—	
...Shepherd	—	—	0 10 0	—	—	—	—	—	—	—	
...nas Steer	6	3/4	—	—	—	—	1 0 0	—	—	—	
...niel Steer	—	1/8	—	—	—	—	0 10 0	—	—	—	
...thur Elliott	—	—	0 10 0	—	—	—	—	—	—	—	
...liam Ezell	—	—	0 10 0	—	—	—	—	—	—	—	
...nnah Pelkin	6	1/4	—	0 8 0	—	—	—	—	—	—	
...a Hall	—	—	—	0 8 0	—	—	—	—	—	—	
...ary Smith	3	—	—	0 4 0	—	—	—	—	—	—	
...rah Lucas	—	—	—	0 4 0	—	—	—	—	—	—	
...arles Meacham	6	2/	—	—	0 12 0	—	—	—	—	—	
...gi Randall	—	—	—	—	0 12 0	—	—	—	—	—	
...d Nye	—	1/10	—	—	0 11 0	—	—	—	—	—	
...mas Hamman	—	1/6	—	—	0 9 0	—	—	—	—	—	
...s. Mitchell	—	1/4	—	—	0 8 0	—	—	—	—	—	
...n Richardson	—	1/2	—	—	0 7 0	—	—	—	—	—	
...vid Dalmon	2	1/10	—	—	1 2 0	—	—	—	—	—	
...nes Edwards	—	2/	—	—	1 4 0	—	—	—	—	—	
...nes Dilloway	4	1/8	to have 2/ a week in future	—	2 0 0	—	—	—	—	—	
...nes Hill	—	2/	—	—	—	2 8 0	—	—	—	—	
...n Smith	2	2/	—	—	—	—	1 4 0	—	—	—	
...s. Cooper	5	7	—	—	—	—	—	—	1 5 0	—	
...nge Parker	4	3/4	—	—	—	—	—	2 16 0	—	—	
...m Wachford	—	2/	—	—	—	—	—	2 8 0	—	—	
...m Stevens	—	2/2	—	—	—	—	—	2 12 0	—	—	
...nes Stevens	—	2/	—	—	—	—	—	2 8 0	—	—	
...nes Leggatt	—	—	—	up to 111th	—	—	—	2 8 0	—	—	
...Hambleton	2	1/8	—	—	—	—	—	—	—	1 0 0	
			7 6 0	1 4 0	7 5 0	2 8 0	2 14 0	17 12 0	1 5 0	1 0 0	36 14 0

books which were specially printed for so many of the great houses. Some of the wages were paid for work at more than one of the family homes – at Great Stanhope Street, London, as well as at Petworth, for instance – and pay was given for odd periods. It might be for four, five or thirteen weeks, for seventy-five days or 'on leaving'. The column-headings made it easy to enter payments to all the staff, whether they worked inside or outside the house.

No. of days	Rate of pay	To men and women working in the house	To do in the laundry	Stables and paddocks	Kennels	Lodge keepers	Under game and park keeper

But sometimes things went wrong. It is disappointing to find that the kindly third Earl, who had always been easy with his servants, found at the end of his life that they had been systematically robbing him, and that this discovery may have shortened his life. In the year after his death there was also evidence of trouble below stairs. A scrap of paper, written with difficulty and now only partly legible, records a complaint by a fellow-servant about one of the Petworth pantrymen.

> Concerning John Dine the pantrey man wich he belonges to the White Hart Club the Bigest Blaggards in England and John Dine is at the head of them and another thing he harbers som of them in the Pantrey . . . i have often told him of it the Pantrey ought not to be left which it twas left last night till half past 10 . . . no sir i hav told lord Egremont of this. . . sir you ought to put a stranger in there alltogether unnone to him at wonce sir i let John Dine and Richard-son in at half Past 10 sir I Dont want 2 men in the Pantrey.

A big house and estate like Petworth had a lot of jobs to offer and no lack of applicants to choose from. A letter written by George Wynd-ham a month after the complaint about John Dine the pantry man gives an insight into the considerations which decided how the different jobs were allotted. He writes about a man called Burgess, who 'has already the peculiar smell belonging to a gamekeeper, which is more calculated for outdoor work, than a drawing Room. I shall give him 14s a week House and Garden, and the same Clothes the other keepers get Burgess is *delighted* at the idea of being a gamekeeper.'

George Wyndham, the third Earl's illegitimate son, who became

Lord Leconfield, was as strict as his father had been easy. Neither his children nor his servants were allowed to go into the little town of Petworth, a few yards from his gates. And both he and his wife had a horror of strangers. When Lady Leconfield went to London her carriage and horses travelled with her by train to Victoria station, where she waited till they were ready to carry her to her town house in Grosvenor Place. And to avoid having strangers near her in the train, the upper Petworth servants travelled with her in a first-class carriage so that all the seats were occupied and there was no risk of an unknown passenger joining them.

His parents' horror of strangers was inherited by their son Henry, second Lord Leconfield. His particular phobia was of strange drinking-water, and when he and his family were in London barrels of water were laboriously delivered there from Petworth. This went on until 1895, when the folly of this arrangement was brought home to everyone by the death of Lord Leconfield's son George – from typhoid fever contracted at Petworth.

There is an unusual record of the looks and personalities of the Petworth servants in the years just following the middle of the century. In 1860 Lord Leconfield's daughter-in-law made a little album containing some thirty photographs of 'the dear Servants at Petworth', and she annotated most of them with reminiscences and descriptions. Photography was a new invention then, and both pictures and notes prove that there was an affectionate relationship between the family and their staff. All the photographs are carefully posed; the servants wear formal, not in the least workaday clothes, and are often seen with the same marble-topped table, a pot plant, and a book or two in the picture.

The album tells of two below-stairs marriages. Mrs Smith, the housekeeper, a dignified figure in cap and dark bombazine dress, had been a Mrs Longford until she married Peter Smith the bailiff, who is seen seated, with high boots and a stick. He was a Cumberland man and was known at Petworth as Cumberland Smith to distinguish him from a second Mr Smith, bailiff and manager of one of the home farms, who cuts a fine figure in high buttoned boots – or are they gaiters? – with his top hat and gloves on the table alongside.

The second bridegroom was Owen, for many years groom of the chambers and afterwards butler and valet to Lord Leconfield. He married 'Tompy', Mrs Thomas, after she had served for many years as

'The dear servants at Petworth' in 1860, from a family photograph album.
(Above left: George Dilloway, park keeper; above right: Dalmon, keeper of the
stallion; below left: Adsett, keeper; below right: Reynolds, laundry maid)

maid to the daughter-in-law who put together the album of servants' photographs. The portrait of Mrs Bowler, who had been the children's nurse, carries a note that '*dear* old Bowler' afterwards became a monthly nurse, and saw all the ladies of the family through their confinements.

Mrs Greenfield, in her full-sleeved dark dress, studiously holding a book in her hand, has hardly the appearance that might be expected of a dairy maid. Nor for that matter is Reynolds, a thoughtful-looking lady in an embroidered, elegantly fitting silk dress, leaning her elbow on two large volumes, a likely-looking laundry maid. There must have been some careful changing out of working clothes before the Petworth staff faced up to the camera. Mr Baubbit was French cook at Petworth for many years after starting as a boy in the kitchen there and later learning from a trained French chef. For his photograph he wore a formal dark suit and his hand rests on the inevitable heavy volume on the marble-topped table.

The outdoor staff look less improbable. Mr Hayward, for many years bailiff and land valuer, is a dignified figure, sitting with walking-stick and bowler hat in hand. He was a Baptist, an honest and capable man who died at a great age. Phillips, who had a long innings as Lord Leconfield's coachman, is in full fig with top hat, boots and whip, Then there is the pad groom, who walked alongside the horses, and the headmaster-like, bearded figure of Gibson the stud groom. Hunting was important at Petworth. Shepherd, for many years the huntsman, is seen with whip and cap; and George Dilloway, park keeper at one of the lodges, hunted the pack of Clumber spaniels and has one of them with him in his photograph.

Petworth, with its large park, rich game reserves and famous deer, employed several keepers. The head keeper lived at the lodge near the deer paddock, and there is a photograph of another keeper, Adsett, a fine old man in a velvet jacket with buttoned waistcoat and boots, holding his cap and stick. He could not read or write and the family reckoned that that was why he was the only keeper who was always able to give an accurate account of the number of birds he had reared. Another genial figure, seen holding a whip and bridle, is Dalmon, keeper of the stallion. He looked after the famous horse 'Whalebone' throughout his life, loved talking of his exploits, and treasured an outline of his hoof which he had traced on a board. Last of the outdoor staff to appear in the Petworth album is Jones, head gardener there for several years before leaving to be the Queen's gardener at Windsor, where he died in her service.

The photographs date from 1860. Twelve years later there were thirty-four indoor staff, with yearly pay varying from £120 for the all-important cook, to a humble £8 for housemaids who were still learning their job. They are all methodically listed:

	Pounds per annum
House Steward	105
Cook	120
Butler	70
Valet	60
2 Under-Butlers	34 and 25
Usher	34
3 Footmen	32, 32, and 28
Lampman	28
Steward's Room Boy	18
Roasting Cook	35
Sculleryman	35
Housekeeper	52 10s
Confectioner	35
5 Laundrymaids	25, 19, 17, 14, and 12
9 Housemaids	23 2s, six at 16 two at 8
2 Kitchenmaids	18 and 12
Stillroom maid	14
Assistant confectioner	10

Servants had to be clothed as well as fed and housed, of course. Livery included hats, gloves, stockings, and pumps, and in 1873 the yearly cost of full Wyndham livery, which was blue with silver crested buttons, came to £34 for the under-butler, £32 each for the footmen, and £28 for the lamp man, while half-liveries cost nearly as much, at £34 for the usher, £18 for the steward's room men, and £25 for the assistant under-butler.

Mrs Smith's Cashbook

Among the Petworth House papers is the cashbook kept by Mrs Smith, the housekeeper in the 1860 album who married Peter Smith the bailiff. She made almost daily entries. Buttons, cotton reels, and pin-papers were bought by the dozen, bed lace by the gross, wadding by the sheet, carpet thread by the pound, and sewing silk by the ounce. She took fifty-four yards of calico at a time, and ordered ninety-six knife-cloths, one hundred and forty-four yards of blind lace, dozens of tea-cloths and twelve pounds of cotton wool.

There must be few people today who can explain what use Mrs Smith made of some of her purchases. Swanskin at 4s 6d, float lace at fifteen pence, and drabbet were all used. So was extra stout green baize, tapestry canvas, a coarse material called crash, holland linen, oiled tabling, marking cotton, silk gimp, scarlet braid, book and fancy muslin, linen tick and linen butts, thread, China silk, loom sheeting, window union, and both sofa and papering canvas.

The Big Account Books

The Petworth account books record the wide range of goods and skills that were needed in the house and on the estate. Expenses during the first quarter of the nineteenth century include bell-hanging, collar-making (for the farms, workmen, dog kennels and gardens), coopery (making casks and barrels), gaiters and gloves ('for his Lordship and the young gentlemen'), and millwright's work ('for the Engine'). An alphabetical 'sundries list' tells of china and chairs to be mended, cider to be made and pressed, and coppers, casks, Daffy's elixir, butter of antimony, buttonhooks, flax seed, grease, Hollands gin, liquorice powder, lemon acid, logwood (the product of a West Indian tree which was used in dyeing), laudanum, oil and conserve of roses, ratty powder, toothbrushes, starch, vermicelli, whiting, truffles, and yeast, to be bought.

There were special accounts, too. Stationery included books and binding, hair-powder (worn by livery servants), ink, India rubber, pencils, pens and quills, sealing-wax, wafers, and steel wire. The eleven gamekeepers needed flints, gunpowder, shot, and paper. Gum dragon, or tragacanth, was used for pharmacy and calico-printing, while from antlers of red deer they concocted oil, sal volatile, and spirits of hartshorn, which contained ammonia. Teapot tin, resin, salt-bay (made from evaporated sea-water), salt-petre (used medicinally as well as for gunpowder and in preserving meat), matches, ochre, pitch, tar, tobacco and pipes, hops and malt were all regularly entered.

Candles were an important item. The cheaper, everyday ones were made of tallow and smelled unpleasantly of animal fat. The best candles were of wax, and much more expensive. At Petworth in 1812, one hundred and thirty-four dozen tallow candles were bought at a cost of about twelve shillings a dozen, as well as sixty-four dozen wax candles at just over two pounds a dozen. Three years later they were using many more – a hundred and eighty-two dozen tallow candles and a hundred and twenty-six dozen wax ones.

Most of the Petworth accounts were kept in massive leather tomes with separate entry lists for the housekeeper, kitchen, baker, confectioner, and gamekeeper. The main expenditure was made by the housekeeper, who bought her goods in bulk. In 1834 her daily needs included:

    4 quarts of groats [hulled oats]
    12 pounds of salt butter
    6 hair brooms
    6 banister brushes
    6 flint mouth brushes
    1 flint crewet [*sic*]
    2 spitting pots
    6 best mops [she had another six four weeks later,
        and again a month after that]
    ½ lb beeswax [for polishing wood]
    12 lbs Fuller's earth [for cleaning and thickening cloth]
    3 gallons of salt
    1 lb of Windsor soap
    6 large stone jars
    5 dozen long gooseberry corks
    6 dozen short gooseberry corks.

For the kitchen, vinegar and salt were purchased by the gallon, and raisins and currants eighty-four pounds at a time. There is not a very clear dividing line between stores for the kitchen and for the confectioner, as his purchases included muscatel raisins, Jordan almonds, gum Arabic, caraway seeds, spices, treacle, and cakes of chocolate. The gamekeeper's needs were concise and down-to-earth: a dozen fish-hooks, fifty flints, gunpowder, and bag shot.

In the 1870s the big house had accounts with a great many specialist tradesmen. As well as run-of-the-mill payments to the butcher, grocer, baker, and newsagent, others were made to the carrier, the butterman, the wax chandler (his was the biggest bill), dressing-case maker, saddler, wine merchant (another heavy item), printer, turner, chimney-sweep, brazier, twiner, surgeon, tea dealer, lamp oil dealer, brewer, kindlers, librarians, bleachers, and the gas company. Payments were made for brougham and piano hire, and for ice. In 1879, £7,471 was paid in tradesmen's bills and £1,879 in servants' wages.

The Petworth farm sent large consignments of produce to the house. In one week in January 1876 the dairy sent up forty-seven pints of cream, a hundred and thirty-eight pints of new milk, a hundred and thirty-four pints of skimmed milk, and seventy-six pounds of fresh butter, as well as some salt butter. The farm supplied thirty-six chickens, fifty-four pounds of pork, two turkeys, and forty eggs. All these items were priced and paid for, and the usual records were kept of the numbers catered for – family, visitors and servants of visitors, and the Petworth establishment.

The estate produced game as well as poultry, meat, and dairy goods. The printed consumption books allow for daily entries of game delivered and kept, and record vast numbers of blackcock, grouse, pheasant, partridge, woodcock, snipe, wild duck, widgeon, teal, plover, hare, and rabbit which found their way to the larder.

The Birthday Party

So much for accounts and produce books. The spirit of Petworth in its heyday also comes across vividly in Greville's description of one of its most festive celebrations. This was a mammoth birthday feast given by the popular old third Earl in 1834, three years before he died. Greville describes how 'fifty-four tables, each fifty feet long, were placed in a vast semicircle on the lawn before the house'. There were two huge tents for the provisions, which were brought in carts, like ammunition. Plum puddings and loaves were piled like cannon-balls, and countless joints of boiled and roast beef were offered when the firing of guns announced that the feast had begun.

Some four thousand tickets were given, but Lord Egremont gave orders that everyone who turned up should be admitted. Local gentry were enlisted to carve the joints, and it was reckoned that in all about six thousand people were fed. There was a band, followed by fireworks, and before the day was over ten thousand people had come together at Petworth. A thousand yards of table-cloth were bought for the occasion, and for the dinner eleven hundred stone of meat, and a thousand plum puddings were provided, as well as quantities of bread, potatoes, salad, and 'abundance of beer'.

7

Wilton House

THE HERBERTS
and their house in Wiltshire

By the first years of the nineteenth century, Wilton had already survived several metamorphoses and there was soon to be yet another. The first Earl of Pembroke had built a Tudor house on the site of the original Saxon abbey, and the next important changes to both house and gardens came in the 1630s, and again some twenty years later, when Inigo Jones was among those who advised on the rebuilding that was needed after a disastrous fire.

During the second half of the eighteenth century, the tenth Earl abandoned his wife and family and eloped to the Continent, siring several illegitimate children and squandering the family fortune. He suggested a classic solution to the problem: his son George must marry an heiress – 'a thirty thousand pounder', as he succinctly put it. When George decided instead to marry his delightful but impecunious cousin, his father found it difficult to share their joy. 'You know', he wrote to his son, 'how very much the situation of our affairs stand in need of at least thirty thousand pounds. I now fear them irretrievable for our time, at least.'

But he was mistaken. When George succeeded his father in 1794, he set to work to put his house, gardens, and estate, as well as his finances, in good order. Wilton was then very uncomfortable and awkward to run, and George was glad to accept the plans of James Wyatt, the most eminent architect of the day, who hoped to 'give a large house the convenience and comfort of a small one'. The eleventh Earl was a determined and methodical man, and he punctiliously kept every bill, receipt, and letter, and also knew what all his staff earned and how much they were each allowed for clothing and travel. His detailed, almost pernickety, instructions, written in his own (often baffling) hand for each of his servants, are the main source for the contents of this chapter.

His marriage did not last long. George's wife died after the birth of their fourth child, and in 1808 he married again. This time his bride was twenty-four years younger than her husband, and was the daughter of the former Russian Ambassador to London. They had five daughters and one son, the able and conscientious Sidney Herbert.

But the eleventh Earl had not solved all his problems. Robert, his son and heir, was following in his grandfather's footsteps, gallivanting wildly on the Continent. In 1814 he clandestinely married a Sicilian princess many years older than himself, and after he succeeded his father, in 1827, he decided to spend the rest of his life abroad. The young Sidney Herbert remembered how the house and family affairs had suffered during his grandfather's absence, and he agreed with his half-brother that he would look after Wilton for him and would make it his home for the rest of his life.

He was true to his word. From 1832 to 1860, Sidney Herbert was a member of Parliament and held several key jobs, including the gruelling one Secretary for War during the Crimean campaign, when he was unfairly blamed for the dreadful sufferings of the army at Sebastopol. In 1860 he was raised to the peerage as Baron Herbert of Lea, but by then he was exhausted by his intolerable burden of work and anxiety, and a year later he died. Soon after that, the twelfth Earl also died, in Paris, and Sidney's two sons succeeded him in turn.

Lord Pembroke's Orders

The Wilton archives have little to tell about the everyday running of the Herberts' magnificent house and estate during the nineteenth century, but the eleventh Earl's unusually detailed notes to his servants about their duties do give a clear picture of how they worked, dressed, and lived. They are headed *Orders for the Servants at Wilton House,* and start by listing the male staff. These were: Henry Coward, the steward; Peritendre, or Peintendre, Lord Pembroke's valet-de-chambre; a butler; a groom of the chambers, who had a German name which is not easy to read – perhaps Bottner; an under-butler; Lord Pembroke's footman; Nathaniel Townshend, the porter; and James, the steward's room man.

The women servants were captained by Elizabeth Stephen, the housekeeper, who was answerable to the steward for her team's 'Good Behaviour, Exactness and Cleanliness'. Then there were Lady Pembroke's maid, her under-maid, the cook, kitchen maid, still-room maid, baking maid, upper- and under-laundry maids, and the upper, second, and third housemaids. The third staff department was the stable, which included a fine riding school, the *manège* – a light, airy place, bigger than many a parish church. The staff here were two coachmen-postilions, Lady Pembroke's groom, the *manège* stable groom, the stud groom, the carter, and a helper.

The steward was the most important member of the staff and was responsible for all the menservants and, through the housekeeper, for the women as well. He waited at table whenever there were more than ten at midday dinner or evening supper. The butler waited at all meals, and the valet-de-chambre waited at midday dinner and, except when Lord Pembroke needed him somewhere else, at the evening supper too. He answered Lord Pembroke's bell at all times. The footmen took turns at waiting duty, and whenever a footman was needed to go out with a carriage the one who was not on duty would go. The under-butler's job is less clear; he never waited at meals or went out with a carriage, 'as he ought to be sufficiently employed at home'. The porter waited at dinner when there were more than ten at table, and whenever this occurred the butler sent word to him that he was to be on duty.

When two carriages were needed a footman went with one and a stable man with the other. The footman escorted the carriage which was going the shortest distance while the stable man – or sometimes Lady Pembroke's groom on his hack – attended the other. So the footman would not be taken away from his work in the house for too long. When one carriage went out with a saddle horse, the coachman or a postilion went with it. The *manège* groom trotted alongside Lord Pembroke whenever he went riding, and he also went with Lady Pembroke if her groom was ill.

Servants' meals at Wilton were served in two sessions. The steward presided over one, while the cook commanded the second table in the servants' hall, where all the livery servants and the laundry, still-room, and other maids dined. Stable staff were on board wages and provided for themselves, which meant that there was no need to prepare meals for their opposite numbers who came with visiting guests, except for those on short visits who took only one meal at the house.

Economy Cuts

Another carefully written paper must be later, as it mentions that Peritendre had been in Lord Pembroke's service for some time and must now be dismissed. As the Herberts divided their time between

Wilton, London, and Pembroke Lodge, their home in Richmond Park, Surrey, staff arrangements had to be planned for all three houses, and this paper is written with London as well as Wilton in mind.

It seems that staff and supplies had been extravagantly used, and it was now necessary to reorganize things and to economize. By this time there were nine menservants – a butler and under-butler, a footman each for Lord and Lady Pembroke, two coachmen, a porter, and, for part of the year, two chair men. The six women servants were the cook-housekeeper, her kitchen-maid, Lady Pembroke's maid, two housemaids, and a laundry maid.

The butler had now stepped into the steward's shoes as comptroller of the household. He must be an Englishman, and was 'to serve as groom of the chambers . . . and to have the entire Direction' of all the staff, though when the family were at Wilton he was not quite such an autocrat. Lord Pembroke's footman had to know how to dress hair, and to act as both footman and valet-de-chambre. The cook-house-keeper had enough to do without extra duties outside her kitchen, but it was her job to keep an eye on the maids and to take care of the linen. One housemaid went with the family when they moved from one of their houses to another, Lady Pembroke's maid washed handkerchiefs, and one laundry maid was now 'quite sufficient, as much less Linnen [sic] need be used, than is at present'.

There is a suggestion that there had been some disagreements among the stable staff, and the new instructions state clearly that the first coachman was to be entirely responsible for the care of the coach horses, and the second coachman to be 'totally under his Direction. No orders to be given to the second when the first is present.' The chair men were now to be engaged and paid by the week and not 're-tained when totally unnecessary, which has often happened.' Another economy would be made whenever Lord Pembroke wanted to have two saddle horses with him; the groom would bring these from the four or five horses in the *manège* stable at Wilton, and would avoid a useless extra expense as well as disputes 'about going fast and slow, far and near'. And a couple of coach horses should be trained to draw a two-or four-wheeled chaise instead of keeping one or two horses and a groom all the year round for that use alone, which was 'quite ridiculous'. There is an unmistakable note of exasperation in Lord Pembroke's plans for his economies.

145

FLUNKEIANA.

John Thomas. "YES, I MUST LEAVE. YOU SEE, MARY, MY DEAR—THERE'S TOO MUCH RED IN THE LIVERY, AND THAT DON'T SUIT MY COMPLEXION—NEVER DID!"

FLUNKEIANA.

Lady's-Maid. "WELL, I'M SURE, MR. ROBERT! I THINK YOU MIGHT FIND SOMETHING BETTER TO DO THAN LOLLOPING ABOUT THAT GREAT EASY CHAIR. YOU MIGHT GO AND HELP IN THE HAY-FIELD, ONE WOULD THINK!"

Flunkey. "OH, YES! AND A NICE FIGGER *I* SHOULD BE! WOT WOULD MISSUS SAY, PRAY, IF I WENT AND SPYLED MY C PLEXION, AND MADE MY 'ANDS 'ARD?"

Staff Comings and Goings

The new régime meant discharging eight servants and engaging three new ones. The ones to go were Peritendre, Michelino, Bottner, the housekeeper, cook, one laundry maid, Lady Pembroke's second maid, and the Swiss boy. In their place they would need a footman for Lord Pembroke, a butler and a cook-housekeeper.

Economies could be made without being ungenerous. Because Peritendre and Michelino had been in Lord Pembroke's service for many years they were allowed £20 and £10 a year respectively. This would save Lord Pembroke about £40 a year,

> with the additional satisfaction of having a Servant of use, whereas at present other Servants are eternally called in to do the Business of the present Incumbents and consequently obliged to neglect their own and Lady Pembroke, who never ought to be neglected ... Lord Pembroke's Income may afford the above Establishment if Economy is strictly attended to, but it will not otherwise.

That led to more dangerous subjects:

> Lady Pembroke must not be moving backwards and forwards, but must settle for Months in some Place or other, many supernumerary wants must be laid aside by her, and no Packets and Parcels must be sent by Land or Water Carriage. Neither Lord Pembroke nor Lady Pembroke must be eternally sending out trifling Messages; Lord Pembroke must appropriate a certain sum annually to himself as Pocket Money, out of which he will pay his Musical People, personal Tradespeople such as Shoemaker, and Travelling Expences. ... Lord Pembroke must not by words or by his manner encourage the Servants in Irregularities of any kind.

The eleventh Earl was determined to keep his side of the bargain. 'Lord Pembroke must begin by putting his part of the Establishment on the footing before-mentioned. ... If he does not begin by doing that, Lady Pembroke cannot be expected to submit to her part.' This was followed by another paper in his handwriting. It settled that if Lord Pembroke had a coachman and a groom in attendance on him, and also enjoyed the Wilton *manège* horses, the stud, and shooting, then Lady Pembroke should have her two maids, two footmen, coachman, postilion, and groom, as well as four coach and two saddle horses. Was it perhaps Lady Pembroke, and not her husband, who

Two cartoons from *Punch*, which   147
illustrate the servants' hierarchy

worded the next sentence? 'If the latter is not allowed to Lady Pembroke, it is to be hoped that Lord Pembroke will not be unmanly enough to take the former for himself. Lord Pembroke must not be keeping up a second Establishment at Wilton or anywhere else.'

Lord and Lady Pembroke were not often together at Wilton. From January until June Lady Pembroke was in town, and from then till September she was at Richmond. She spent the whole of September and October at Wilton, and the last two months of the year at Richmond or London as she pleased. In town, of course, life was more formal and ceremonious. All livery servants and maids were given a knife, fork, and spoon to keep for their own use, and they had to replace these if they were lost or damaged. There was also a protocol for complaints: these were not to be made directly to Lord or Lady Pembroke. Menservants were to make their complaints to the butler, and it was he who mentioned such things, if he considered this necessary, to Lady Pembroke. Complaints from women servants would be heard by the housekeeper. The only case when a grumble was reported at first-hand to the Pembroke family was when a servant had a complaint to make against the butler. On such occasions Lord Herbert would be the one to listen and adjudicate.

Livery and Wages

The Earl was also careful to give clear orders about the handing out of livery to his servants. Every third of June the butler handed the porter, footman, under-butler, coachman, and groom a blue frock, a waistcoat, a pair of black breeches and a 'round silver-laced Patent Hatt'. It was a busy day for the butler, as he also gave each of them a complete livery suit, and issued splendid hats and cockades to the grooms and coachman. All were to be worn on 4 June, the King's birthday.

These fine feathers were not allowed to lie around and get spoiled. On 5 June the butler checked that all were clean and in good trim, and took them back. Six months later, in mid-January, out came the livery and hats again, and were given to the servants, while the porter, footman, and under-butler were presented with new working-frocks. The under-butler had a leather apron as well. The 'stable people' were given new working-frocks, stable waistcoats, trousers, and smock frocks. Each servant had a great coat, and a box cloak was provided every other year for Lord and Lady Pembroke's carriages. As a general rule servants wore livery in town and frocks in the country. It was the butler's responsibility to make sure that clothes were tried on in good time to be altered, if necessary, before the delivery date.

Wages were paid half-yearly, and other expenses were settled every Monday. These included the flambeaux to light servants on their way as they escorted the family through the dark London streets, and payments to the chair men who carried Lady Pembroke's sedan. Servants left in town when the family were not at home were paid nine shillings a week board wages; a bonus payment raised this to half a guinea for the upper servants. An extra shilling a day was allowed to every servant who was asked to travel. All payments were methodically entered and receipts were duly given for wages paid.

The butler was responsible for paying bills. When he was in town he went to market every morning and paid cash for everything he bought. Other bills were paid twice a year. The butler kept a daily account book which he carried with him wherever he went and he showed it, together with the cellar book, to Lady Pembroke at a fixed time every morning.

Managing the Wilton Estate

Gradually the eleventh Earl managed to get his establishments and finances in order again. In 1809 Farington reported that Lord Pembroke was then living in apartments on the ground floor at Wilton, sedulously avoiding any ostentation or display, and occasionally using one or two small rooms on the first floor. All his affairs were entrusted to an agent called John Seagrim, who received all monies on his master's behalf, entered them in his cash book, and made all payments for the proper management of the estates. Nobody else had any hand in the Earl's business affairs.

Seagrim managed all lettings and rents, and had special instructions to cut down 'the Arrears, which are now become enormous, and amount nearly to the Sum of £2,000'. He paid the wages of all workmen and labourers each week, and was careful that only those who were 'absolutely necessary and consistent with strict Economy' were taken on. He was paid a salary of £120 a year, with an additional

£15 a month for his expenses 'on near journeys', and to help him with his work he had a clerk. The Earl wrote out further instructions when Seagrim was about to marry, and a note was included to confirm that he would be allowed £12 a year for house rent, because it would not be convenient for him to live at Wilton House. But all eventualities were provided for, and Seagrim's briefing ends on a rather ominous note: 'if by any accident you should hereafter be in a single state, and unencumbered by a Family, you are to reside at Wilton house'.

So the years when the eleventh Earl was master of Wilton were well organized, and slowly but surely the family finances recovered. In August 1819 Farington reported a much more affluent and easy state of affairs. The artist Westmacott had been at Wilton and he found Lord Pembroke living 'with Baronial hospitality. They usually sit down about 22 at dinner, his Lordship sits at the dinner table but a short time after the Ladies retire. He then asks if the Company choose more wine, and the negative being expressed, they adjourn and amuse themselves by driving in Carriages or walking.'

But when the twelfth Earl, who married illicitly in Sicily when he was only twenty-one and settled in France, succeeded in 1827, it seemed once again that Wilton would be neglected and empty, with an uncaring master based abroad. Fortunately the Earl's half-brother, Sidney Herbert, foresaw this danger, and arranged to take on responsibility for Wilton and to live there. He had great care and affection for it, and when he was a boy he wrote from school to his mother that 'there is not a spot about Wilton now which I do not love as if it were a person', and this devotion was shared by his mother and his wife.

Sidney Herbert is said to have treated his servants like members of his family, and to have been unsparing in his care for retired housemaids, carpenters, and estate staff. He died in 1861, and a year later his son became thirteenth Earl. By the late 1860s there was a steady income from visitors who turned up and paid for the privilege of seeing the house. But strangely enough, the Wilton estate accounts show a falling-off in numbers of visitors after that, with entrance money dropping from £50 then to only £20 ten years later. There is no clue as to why this happened, and it is all the more surprising at a time when the railways were making travel easier, and most great houses were attracting ever-increasing streams of visitors.

8

Woburn Abbey

THE RUSSELLS
and their house in Bedfordshire

Like Holkham, Woburn Abbey in the nineteenth century was the home of an eminent Whig family, whose members played active parts in agriculture and public life, and both the house and the park were stately and impressive on the grand scale. 'The whole appears like what it is, the complete establishment of a great lord in this country, without any ostentatious display or ornament' was the verdict of one well-travelled visitor in 1807. There were to be some ups and downs in the years to come, but the description held good for the rest of the century.

There was certainly no lack of space. Two complete sets of rooms allowed alternative summer and winter living quarters, but both were often empty as the family were endlessly on the move and often went to their other homes – in Bedfordshire, Devon, Cambridgeshire, and Surrey, as well as London. Already in the eighteenth century, there had been some useful rebuilding and modernization, when four pioneer water-closets and a hot bath were added, and the old kitchen and staff quarters were pulled down and replaced. New larders, brewhouses, and laundries helped to lighten the drudgery of the servants, and earthenware stoves were imported from France to relieve the chill of staircases and passages which were outside the range of the blazing wood and coal fires in the great rooms.

During the nineteenth century seven Dukes of Bedford presided at Woburn. The sixth Duke inherited in 1802, when he retired from Parliament so that he could give full attention to the care of his properties. A family man with thirteen children by two marriages, he was an enthusiastic naturalist and collector of paintings and sculpture. His third son was Lord John Russell, later Earl Russell, a leading Whig member of Parliament for forty-seven years, who held many of the highest offices, and was twice Prime Minister.

The sixth Duke enjoyed spending money lavishly, but he inherited daunting liabilities, and he see-sawed strangely between princely extravagance and petty economies. In 1820 Greville wrote enthusiastically about a visit to Woburn, and it is worth remembering that his was the admiration of a man who was accustomed to visiting

154

the stateliest of English homes. 'The house, place, establishment and manner of living', he wrote, 'are the most magnificent I have seen. There is no place which gives so splendid an example of a Great English Lord as this.' But there were signs that it was not altogether easy for the Duke to provide such lavish hospitality. At one great dinner, served on gleaming ancestral plate by servants in rose-coloured coats and white breeches, one of the guests recognized the man who marked the Duke's tennis court among the assistants out of livery who were helping to wait at table.

And when the Duke invited his son William to bring his family to Woburn he made it clear that he could offer them no more than 'beef or mutton, cabbage and potatoes'. His explanation sounds simple enough. 'I have what is vulgarly called run out in household expenditure, the cause of it housekeeping going on at so many residences.' But he still managed to plant a new maze at his Devonshire home, stocked his greenhouses with choice and costly plants, planned an arboretum, imported acorns from Portugal, and engaged Repton to make a fine new approach to the west front of Woburn. 'I shall have some operose and expensive work going on at Woburn this year, in repairs, painting, etc. etc.,' he wrote to his son in 1826. But the anxiety was still there, and he added that he was 'obliged to economise as much as possible'.

Most of those who knew Woburn in the first forty years of the century were quite unaware of any cheese-paring. The day began with prayers at 9.30 a.m., followed, at ten, by breakfast, where it was an attractive novelty to serve tea instead of beer, and each person was given his own little gold teapot. Dinner was a stately meal of at least nine courses on a table gleaming with silver and china, and with the groom of the chambers, the butler, and footmen in attendance. At the end of the sixth Duke's time, his son noted in his diary that he had been to Woburn and found it 'full of people, twenty-four at table. What splendid luxury, what refinement, what comfort.' And yet something was missing. A few years earlier he had paid another visit to his old home, 'always the most enjoyable of places, yet so little enjoyed by its owners'.

The seventh Duke inherited a heavy load of debts in 1839, and resolved to set his finances in order. Even so, the housekeeper's accounts for the Christmas quarter in 1840 had come to nearly £4,000, although the Duke and his family had spent only five weeks at the

Sheepshearing at Woburn Abbey in 1811 by George Garrard. Thomas Coke of Norfolk was a guest and is one of the figures standing on the right. The Duke of Bedford is mounted in the centre

house. And they managed a royal reception for the young Queen and Prince Albert the following year, with the Duke of Wellington, Lord Melbourne, and Lord and Lady Palmerston also among the guests. That Christmas the Duke's sister wrote to a friend, describing the splendour of the new régime at Woburn.

> In point of magnificence it is equal to the old days, & in point of comfort there is evident improvement; that is, all that concerns the housekeeper's department is more *soigné*. We are 30 at table, great profusion, & an admirable *cuisine*, besides repasts at every hour of the day. From 10 to 12 breakfast – from 2 to 3 luncheon, from 5 to 6 tea, at 7 dinner, & after balls & theatres hot suppers, otherwise cold.

By then Greville had enjoyed Woburn hospitality for more than twenty years, so he also could compare the seventh Duke's reign with his father's. His verdict was enthusiastic.

> The Duke is well and wisely administering his estate and improving his magnificent palace in every way. I never saw such an abode of luxury and enjoyment, one so full of resources for all tastes. The management of his estates is like the administration of a little kingdom. He has 450 people in his employment on the Bedfordshire property alone, not counting domestic servants. His pensions amount to £2,000 a year. There is order, economy, grandeur, comfort and general content.

A few years later, after another visit, Greville endorsed his first impression of the seventh Duke's way of life, and described some of the skilled labour that made it possible.

> Such magnificence in House, Park, and gardens, such buildings all over the estate, farmhouses fit for gentlemen and intended for men of education and knowledge, vast workshops where everything is done that is required for the property, carpenters, ironmongers, painters, and glazers, three hundred artificers in the employment of the Duke, and paid every Saturday night . . . the consequence is that the Duke of Bedford is every day making his colossal fortune greater and greater.

There was a third occasion when Greville was impressed by Woburn in the seventh Duke's time. One morning in 1852, when the hounds met there 'and there was half the county at breakfast in the great Hall', the Duke was called away for a more important matter. He had to see a messenger, sent to him from the Queen at Osborne House.

The seventh Duke was succeeded in 1861 by his son, a bachelor and a recluse, who handed over the management of all his estates to his cousin (later the ninth Duke). This he undertook courageously and efficiently, and he used to say that he had known what it was to live at different times on £200 a year and on £200,000. He had been a reluctant Member of Parliament, and his main interest was in agricultural experiments, many of which he launched at Woburn. He was a hypochondriac and, some twenty years after he succeeded, he went mad and shot himself. The last two nineteenth-century Dukes of Bedford were his sons.

The Servants

At the beginning of the century there were sixteen menservants at work in the Abbey, as well as thirty-two on outside jobs, and twenty-nine in the gardens. Those inside the house were the house steward, butler, valet, two grooms of the chambers, cook (with a French surname), usher of the hall, under-butler, four footmen, a waiter in the steward's room, baker, house porter, and a man who doubled up on the jobs of lamplighter and watchman. Outside there were two gate porters, an office lodge-keeper, and an office porter and watchman, a park keeper, and two gamekeepers. The chief groom had seven grooms and six helpers in the stables, to look after the Duke's thirty-four riding and carriage horses, and there was a whipper-in and another helper to manage the pack of harriers and twenty other dogs. There were two coachmen and five postilions for the eleven Woburn carriages. Six of these were four-wheelers—a *vis à vis*, a coach, a chariot, a postchaise, a barouche, and a phaeton – while the curricle and two gigs had only a pair of wheels apiece. There were also two wagons or brakes. It is interesting that most of the elaborate carriages have French names, whereas there were English reach-me-down terms for the humbler, everyday ones.

Sixty years later, in the 1860s, the inside staff had not changed much, though by then there was an additional letter-carrier, a second 'in watchman', an accountant, a sculleryman, a laundryman (who

A List of the greatest Number of Male Servants, Horses, Carriages, Dogs &c.ª kept by His Grace The Duke Of Bedford, between the 5.th of April 1804 and the 5.th of April 1805 —

1	Zacharias Hancock	- - -	House Steward
2	John Barling	- - - -	Butler
3	Francis Williams	- -	Valet
4	Henry Herbert	}	Grooms of the Chambers
5	Benjamin Baudd		
6	John Roviere	- -	Cook
7	Robert Chance	- - -	Usher of the Hall
8	John Wooldin		Under Butler
9	James Bishop	}	
10	Richard Outon		Footmen
11	James Smith		
12	John Skampton		
13	Robert Savage		Waiter in Stewards Room
14	James Fleet		Baker
15	James Godfrey		House Porter
16	William Henley		Lamplighter & Watchman
17	John Parkins	}	Gate Porters
18	Mich.ᵉ Boulsover		
19	John Key		Office Lodge Keeper
20	James Keffar		d.º Porter & Watchman
21	William Elder	}	Coachmen
22	Henry Walker		
23	William Watkins		
24	Edward Bailey	}	
25	John Townsend		Postillions
26	William King		
27	Thomas Sear		

(turn over)

| 28 | John Marsden | — | Chief Groom & Huntsman |

29	William Blanchett
30	Joseph Marshall
31	Richard Gardner
32	William Stow	— Grooms —
33	Thomas Dinn
34	James Lancaster
35	Henry Sharp

36	Richard Grace
37	Sam¹ Tebby
38	Mich¹ Ramsden
39	John Row	Helpers in Stables
40	Ezekiel Weafer
41	Thomas Henley

| 42 | John Smith | — — — | Whipper-in |

| 43 | Thomas Darling | — | Helper in Kennel |

| 44 | William Bullock | — | Park-keeper |

45	George Bowdler
46	John Brookes	Gamekeepers at Woburn
47	John Peet	d° — at Thornhaugh

| 48 | Samuel Martin |
| 49 | John Dowdall | Gardeners — |

27 Men employed in the Gardens under them

Total 49 Servants,

Carriages with 4 Wheels —

1 Vis a Vis	1 Post Chaise
1 Coach	1 Barouch
1 Chariot	1 Phaeton —

6 Total

Carriages with 2 Wheels —

1 Curricle — 2 Gigs —

2 Waggons or Breaks — which pay no Duty —

The Duke of Bedford does not consider himself liable chargeable for any
Gamekeeper but which as he says were etc

stuck it out for thirty years at a weekly wage of eighteen shillings), and a man who came five times a year to do the brewing. The women servants, under the all-powerful housekeeper, were a confectioner, three laundry maids, two kitchen-maids, six housemaids, a still-room maid, two needlewomen, and two charwomen. The stable staff had shrunk surprisingly, and now consisted only of a coachman, two grooms, a maid, and a man who came to clean the rooms.

The house steward headed the Woburn menservants and was responsible for them all, as well as for the wine cellar and for all produce from the dairy, the kitchen garden, and the game department, whether this was earmarked for the Abbey or for sending away. His second-in-command was the groom of the chambers, who at Woburn had the special job of superintending all meals at the Duke's table. He also stage-managed the endless comings and goings to and from the house and looked after the 'important' writing-tables, leaving the minor ones to the footmen. The usher of the hall – among other duties – saw to it that the many lamps and lampshades were clean and in good trim. Yardmen kept the scores of coal-scuttles and log-baskets filled. Also on the staff-list, although in no sense a domestic servant, was the house clerk; he did all the office work, paid bills and wages, gave orders to tradesmen and suppliers for goods required at the Abbey and the stables, and also did such useful odd jobs as looking up times of trains. The weighbridge clerk was responsible for coal, wood, charcoal, and suchlike supplies, as well as for packages coming to and from the house.

The kitchen was a department on its own, with a head cook (male) who was accountable only to the house clerk and to the Duke. He had under-cooks to help him, and there was also – because of the Woburn system of keeping all servants on board wages – a cook specially for the servants' hall. For some reason, what in many houses was called the still-room was known there as the confectioner's office. Another responsible job was that of master of the stables, and the last holder of this title lived on, full of years but no longer with any work to do, until nearly the middle of the present century.

The great ledger in which the Woburn servants' register was methodically kept has ten columns on each page. These were for entries of each person's name, home address, date of entering the Duke's service, rate of wages, amount of board wages, washing allowance, yearly total, date of any increases, date of leaving, and any personal records or remarks. It shows that those who rose to the top jobs – the housekeeper, the house steward, first housemaid, butler, groom of the chambers, and usher of the hall – were happy to stay on for years. But many of the others – under-housemaids, first and second kitchen-maids, scullery and laundry maids – moved off fairly quickly, unless they were either promoted or married one of the menservants who worked in the house or on the estate. As at many other great houses, servants were often recruited from the nearby village, and sons and daughters of staff were given the chance of getting a foot on the ladder by being taken on as yard boys or laundry maids. Long years of service with the family were rewarded by pensions, and sometimes a rent-free house on the estate.

Elizabeth Payne, a Woburn woman, held the top job of housekeeper for nearly thirty years, starting in 1865. She was seventy-four when she left, and was given a pension amounting to the total of her earnings and board wages, and she also had £100 from the previous Duke. A year after her departure her place was filled by the first housemaid. Graduating from under-housemaid to first housemaid, and then to housekeeper at one or other of the family houses, was a good way for a local girl to 'better herself'. The Woburn servants' register tells of one under-housemaid who worked well for three years, was then given an encouraging wage increase, but left soon afterwards to marry a stableman. Another was taken on as under-housemaid at Woburn after three years in service with the Duchess of Buccleuch; she worked her way up to the position of first housemaid, and was eventually promoted to be housekeeper at another house belonging to the family, some twelve miles from Woburn.

Then there was an under-housemaid who got her promotion, was sent to work at the Belgrave Square house for two years, came back to Woburn, and four years later married the Duke's under-valet. But sometimes even a good housemaid had to wait a long time for recognition. Mary Price came from the Eaton Square household in 1877 and worked as first housemaid for sixteen years for the same wages. After the eleventh Duke succeeded her luck changed, and in two years she had four quick rises, followed by promotion to the job of housekeeper at Belgrave Square the year after.

The first lady's maid was the Duchess's principal maid, personally appointed and paid from her own purse. The entries start in the 1890s, so probably the appointment did not exist before the time of

163

the eleventh Duke. Two of those mentioned were French, one was German, and two others were sisters. None stayed long in the job, which suggests that perhaps the Duchess was an exacting mistress. Laundry maids seem to have been recruited from much further afield than most of the other women servants. Is it fair to guess again that perhaps this was because local girls knew what the job was like and were careful not to apply for it? Their wages were even lower than those of the girls in the scullery, and many of them left after only a few months, although one or two managed to make a success of the job. Hannah Blenkhorn, from Stockton-on-Tees, did two years as laundry maid before being promoted head laundry maid, but she got no further, and five years later she left. And Emily Bellinger worked in the laundry for twelve years without a rise, but then had a lucky year when her pay was doubled and she married a stableman.

The needlewomen were skilled and important people. Maria Brittain started work in 1843 when she was eighteen; thirty years later she was promoted to the job of housekeeper at Endsleigh, the Bedfords' *cottage orné* in Devonshire, and in 1889, when she was sixty-eight, she was finally pensioned-off at £50 a year. When Sarah Holmes started work alongside her in 1860 her £20 a year was less than the head kitchen maid earned, and only just above the housemaids' wages. She stitched away for nineteen years before getting her first £2 rise and her wages crept up by only £5 in the next fourteen years; but after that her thirty-four years of skilled service were rewarded and she went off to Belgrave Square as housekeeper.

John Sprague started work at Woburn in 1836 and stayed on there for over half a century. He was twenty when he came, and he worked his way up from footman and under-butler to the double job of butler and groom of the chambers. He ended up as the all-important house steward, and he seems to hold the record for length and distinction of service. His brother Henry, ten years younger, followed in his footsteps by doing various jobs at the Abbey, ending with nineteen years as groom of the chambers. The men who followed the Spragues moved up the same ladder, learning the job as under-butlers before eventually getting their promotion to house steward.

But the groom of the chambers was not always heading for the heights. Richard Jones had been hall porter in London in his youth and then had various changes of work before taking on the job at Woburn for three years. The next two were both dismissed, one with the brief comment 'not sober'. And of course some men were not ambitious. Charles Flood was content with the job of under-butler at the same pay for forty years; and Henry Arthur, a local man, did the double job of usher of the hall and lamp man for even longer and was rewarded by several rises and a rent-free house. Another long server was the porter at the house, who was given a pension and an annuity in recognition of nearly sixty years' work. For some reason the porters at the lodge had to be tougher characters than those at the house, and were recruited from non-commissioned officers in Guards regiments.

Among the youngest of the Abbey servants were the yard boys, who were taken on at thirteen or fourteen, straight from school. As the years passed their job changed and their time was divided between the confectioner's office and morning and night post duty, so they then came be be known as confectioner's and night post boys. The servants' hall boys were also young, though several had already served as letter-carriers. Promotion for them would be to third under-butler, footman, or steward's room boy, and from there the way lay ahead to the under-butler's job.

From 1862 the house carpenter was Frederick West, who in his later years had his son Francis as his assistant. The Duke apprenticed the boy to some Bedford carpenters before taking him on at Woburn, and eventually, when his father retired on full pay, Francis took over the job, with a free house and clothing allowance to make up for a rather lower wage than his father had been earning.

The 'odd men' were as useful at Woburn as at many other great houses in the last century, and they were prepared to turn their hands to most jobs that needed doing. Francis Fleet had previously worked as a chimney sweep, Zacharias Chapman helped with the hay harvest at the Park Farm during busy times, and Harry Cook had poor health, which handicapped him as a labourer and for work in the kitchen and scullery. But he pulled his weight for twenty years as odd man, and was paid an additional five shillings a week for pumping water every evening.

Night watchmen were needed both outside and inside the house, and would be transferred from the one job to the other as they grew older. They came from other outdoor work and often stayed on for years. Benjamin Taylor was indoor watchman from 1877 to 1894, and Jabez Jones overlapped with him after working as a boy in 'the Park Farm gang', in the dairy, as a labourer in the woods, and as mechanics labourer at the farm. David Dickens had done over thirty years as poultry yard boy and mechanics labourer at the farm before becoming yard man at the house, and eventually indoor watchman. He was finally degraded to yard man for misconduct, but without any reduction in his wages.

Outside in the stables, Marshall Staples, from the village, was coachman from 1857 to 1893. He handed over to an ex-sergeant from a Guards regiment, who had started as helper and then moved up to be groom and under-coachman. There were also the riding grooms, the farrier and saddler, the stablemen – who came and went fairly briskly, many of them being dismissed – and two dog men. The last year of the century marked the start of a new age, when the Duke's 'motor establishment' was manned by one mechanic-cum-motor-driver, and two washers.

Other outdoor staff worked in the gardens, the deer park, and the game and fish departments. One under-keeper did a total of fifty years' service, starting as park labourer and going on to twenty-five years as rabbiter, and nine as watcher. Another came to the job after work in the park, where he made himself useful watching and trapping rooks.

Board Wages, Allowances, and Pensions

Board wages in most great houses were paid only when the family was away from home, but at Woburn they were the rule, and in some cases came to more than a servant earned. The rates were 15s a week for upper servants, while the others had 10s 6d (men) and 9s 6d (maids). In 1865 the housekeeper and the groom of the chambers were both paid quarterly wages amounting to £50 a year, and their 15s weekly board wages were raised to 17s 6d when they went to London. The steward's board wages were the same as theirs, though his annual pay came to £120. Maids were all given an additional sixpence a week for sugar, as well as their 9s 6d board wages, whether they earned £35 a year like the head kitchen maid and the confectioner or £12 like the youngest laundry maid and housemaid. In the same way the under menservants all had their 10s 6d board wages, although their yearly pay ranged from £18 for the scullery man and the steward's room man to the footman's £28 and the under-butler's £31 10s.

At Woburn the system of board wages seems to have misfired.

Visitors grumbled that they could never get anything to eat or drink between meals as all supplies had to be dispensed by the housekeeper for formal dining-room use. 'Woburn is the most uncomfortable house I have ever stayed in,' the Duke's cousin complained. 'If I was dying of starvation I could not get even a biscuit between meals.' And another guest who asked the butler for a cup of tea was told that this could not be as the servants were on board wages and could not be expected to provide visitors with refreshments. This was certainly not the purpose of board wages, and it is not clear why the Woburn arrangements led at times to such stingy housekeeping.

When the family went from Woburn to London the only servants who went with them were the housekeeper, steward, groom of the chambers, under-butler, and footman. On occasions when servants had to travel they were paid set amounts for meals and lodgings. Both upper and under servants were allowed 1s 6d for breakfast and supper 'on the road', but upper servants were paid 3s for their midday meal while under servants had only 2s 6d. And when they stayed more than one night at an inn, upper servants were allowed 5s a night and under servants had 4s 6d.

Washing allowances were paid to all the women servants except the housekeeper, charwomen, and laundry maids, but not to the men except, surprisingly, the Abbey lodge porter. There were also allowances for special needs, as in the case of John Clark, under-keeper and head keeper from 1876 to the end of the century, who was given an extra £15 a year towards the keep of his horse, as well as a man to help him and a special supply of towels.

Stores were given out to the servants at the Abbey every month, and quantities varied according to the time of the year. In the two summer quarters (25 March to 29 September) fourteen candles a month were dealt out to the housemaids, still-room maid, and office maids, and they had twice as many during the winter. They also had a pound and a half of soap, five ounces of starch, and one ounce of 'stone blue' (for laundering) each month. Kitchen-maids were allowed rations of tea and sugar when the family were 'at housekeeping'. The housekeeper doled out a quarter of a pound of tea to each person every week, and the 'man cook' distributed the sugar. The kitchen-maids had to make do with only fourteen candles between the lot of them each month, as it was reckoned that they used oil to light the kitchen, and during the summer they did not need more than six to eight candles a month.

When the family were at the Abbey and there was therefore a full complement of servants there too, the footman, house porter, lamplighter, and house carpenter all converged on the still-room for their tea, which was brewed by the still-room maid. (At this point in the book of rules Mrs Palfreeman, the housekeeper, added a reassuring comment that on these occasions 'the greatest economy is used'.) Tea and sugar for visitors' servants were kept, and accounted for, by the usher of the hall, who also carefully noted down their numbers, and brought his account to the housekeeper every time he came for fresh supplies. The allowance was a quarter of a pound of tea and half a pound of sugar a week for each visiting servant. They took their meals in the two staff dining-rooms according to their jobs – lady's maids and valets in the house steward's room, and footmen in the servants' hall.

The baker was allowed a pound and a half of soap each month and when the family was 'at housekeeping' he also had a pound of tea and two and a half pounds of moist sugar every five weeks. Supplies were allocated to the rest of the servants according to need, with a special extra ration of tea and sugar for the laundry maids because they had to provide for the women who came in to help with the washing – who were up so early that they had to have a second breakfast.

The butler was responsible for the amount of wine allowed to those who took their meals at the house steward's table. One bottle between six people (men and women) was considered enough, with an extra bottle for odd numbers. The list of stores given out to the Woburn staff at this point includes a note that their ration of half a pint of wine each was considerably more than the quantity allowed at Belvoir Castle. On special occasions like Christmas and New Year's Day the ration might be more generous – say, one bottle for four.

As well as vegetables and skimmed milk, servants at the Abbey were allowed regular supplies of ale and beer. Sixteen quarts of table beer went to the laundry maids every day, three to the Abbey lodge-keeper, and two each to the lamplighter (who was night watchman in the house every other week), the outdoor watchman, the chimney-sweeper, and the gardeners who brought vegetables to the house. When servants were living on board wages there were eight quarts of table beer for the housemaids, nine for maids and men working in the kitchen, one for the office maid, and two each for the still-room maid and the house carpenter. The servants went on drinking beer with their breakfast for years after the family and their guests had taken to tea instead. The usher of the hall had the job of going to the cellars in the morning, at noon, and at night to draw the beer.

Staff who took their meals in the servants' hall had no ale allowed to them when they were on board wages, but when 'at housekeeping' they had table beer at dinner and ale after dinner. For this there was no fixed quantity: the usher of the hall drew it, poured it out, and saw to it 'that none take too much and that none get tipsy'. Those who had their meals in the steward's room did better as they had their ration of ale and beer whether they were on board wages or not. Tradesmen from the village occasionally asked for some ale when they called at the Abbey and were then usually given a horn (about half a pint) by the butler or the usher of the hall. Postboys and others who ate in the servants' hall had a pint of ale and a little beer if they wanted it.

The huge pensions which Greville mentioned being paid by the seventh Duke of Bedford were in line with those granted to many Woburn servants on retirement. Unless they had managed to save during their working lives, pensions or poor-law relief were, of course, all they had to look forward to. Pensions seem to have been reviewed by each Duke soon after coming into his inheritance. The ninth Duke paid out about £1,000 in pensions to thirty-two old servants. Three were upper servants, rewarded for years of service with £50 a year each: John Sprague, the house steward, got his when he was seventy-five and already had an annuity under the will of the seventh Duke. His brother Henry, ten years younger, had the same amount, although he had done only nineteen years as groom of the chambers, and was only fifty-eight when he retired. Mary Brittain had done forty-nine years, first as needlewoman and later as housekeeper at Endsleigh, before she was given her pension at the age of sixty-five.

Many of the others on the ninth Duke's pension list were outside staff who had had long working lives. John Bowles had been the Duke's coachman for twenty-one years, and William Sinfield started as groom and went on to be carriage-washer for forty-two years at the Abbey stables. His older brother, James, had served even longer, both as groom and as vermin-killer in the Woburn woods. The longest career of all seems to have been that of James Keens, who began by working in the kitchen gardens, went on to do everyday jobs in the park and woods, and finally chalked up a total of sixty years outside service.

9

Attingham Park

THE BERWICKS
and their house in Shropshire

Attingham Park, a few miles from Shrewsbury, had an exceptionally large number of owners during the nineteenth century. At its start, the second Baron Berwick was master there, and he was succeeded by six others between 1832 and 1897. The house they lived in had been built in the 1780s as a classical addition to a much earlier building, and ambitious changes were made in both the mansion and the park during the next fifty years. By 1827 so much money had been spent on Attingham and on the second Lord Berwick's travels that everything in the house had to be sold, and the place was leased to Lord Berwick's brother until he inherited it five years later. The third Lord Berwick redecorated and refurnished the empty skeleton of Attingham splendidly, and he too was succeeded by his brother. The family papers include some interesting clues to the way the seven owners and their servants lived, and to the tradesmen and craftsmen who worked for them. The detailed catalogue of the 1827 sale is specially interesting as it names and takes us into every room in the house, pointing to each piece of furniture – every pot and pan, every tool, every kitchen or household utensil that was there at the time. Without this, it would not be easy to see how the house was run, as the Berwicks did not play a leading part in public affairs and so do not come to life in the letters and diaries of the day.

The Rooms and What Was in Them

Attingham was planned so that the main rooms of the house were grouped around the central court, a long way from the servants' bedrooms and working quarters. Lord and Lady Berwick had their separate suites – including washing room, dressing room, and morning room – on each of the two corners of the house. The catalogue of the 1827 sale may have over-stated things – sale catalogues often do – but it gives a good picture of the two 'sumptuous lofty double-screwed lath-bottom Four-Post' bedsteads, each with its set of mahogany bed-steps twenty-one inches high. These were made in three tiers with carpeted

The dining room at Attingham, showing the table laid for dinner. Watercolour by Lady Hester Leeke, *c.* 1850

Mounted postilions and a groom at the posting stage in *Gretna Green*, by J. F. Herring, 1846

steps and a box top, and one of the two was fitted with a 'night-convenience'.

Most of the servants' beds were also four-posters and, like the rest of their furniture, were made of deal, beech, or oak. Their bedrooms were in the long staff wing, which had the servants' hall at one end and the laundry and greenhouse at the other. A big bedroom came next to the servants' hall, and the cook's room was between that and the kitchen. Beyond them were other bedrooms, and rooms for the steward and under-steward. Then there were the pastry, the scullery and salting room, the carpenter's store room, and the footman's room. In the basement were a large menservants' dormitory, an under-butler's bedroom, a butler's pantry and sitting-room (with a working pantry adjoining it), a steward's room, and the housekeeper's room. There were more servants' bedrooms upstairs, where the housekeeper's and the lady's maid's rooms had the best furniture. The first housemaid was privileged to have a bedroom to herself with a single four-poster in it, while next door to her the room was shared – and perhaps the two beds too – by several under-housemaids. The back courtyard housed lamp and knife rooms, dairy, bakehouse, wash-house, brew-house, and beer cellars.

Meals in the servants' hall were served on a massive square deal table, and the staff sat down to them on long wooden forms. There was plenty of home-brewed beer, drawn from generous beer-cans holding three, four, or ten quarts, which stood on wooden carriages with wheels. Meals in the steward's room were more elegant and were served on a long mahogany table. Though it was convenient to have the working quarters separate from the rooms where the family lived, this meant that the kitchen was a long way from the dining-room. Wine was carried there in a four-bottle basket, and there were others for plate, as well as special knife and spoon trays. Stores of tea were kept in big round covered canisters, each holding eight pounds, and in wooden tea-chests which had locks and keys, and two caddies so that different kinds of tea could be kept apart. Copper and tin tea-kettles and an imposing tea-urn all had their own stands and lamps. There were pewter ice moulds, freezers, and 'shapes', as well as a hefty square ice trough, lined with lead, with its own cover, standing on stout legs.

A lot of nineteenth-century kitchen equipment was made of wood. At Attingham there was a great round chopping-block, and two large iron-bound, wooden dish tubs. Harder to imagine is the six-foot deal 'panelled meat screen, with hot closet at the top, and iron rack shelves inside', lined with tin, and enclosed by folding doors on rollers. Pails were made of wood and so were laundry-bowls, which had handles. A regiment of gleaming copper pots and pans, meticulously lined up in order of size, formed the impressive *batterie de cuisine*. There were long two-handled turbot kettles with plates and covers, and smaller fish kettles as well. Five ample stock-pots and some thirty stew-pans came in different sizes. Frying-pans, *sauté* pans, baking pans, and omelette pans were not so different from their descendants which are in use today. A stately square dripping-pan stood on its own legs, with a well to collect the fat, and a long-handled ladle to spoon it up for basting. There were other basting ladles and spoons, as well as fish slices, moulds, patty pans, and tart pans.

Some dishes were made of pewter, and there were water-plates to fill with boiling water so that the food on them could be kept hot. 'Tins' were listed separately in the sale catalogue, and included graters, flour cans, dish covers, candlesticks and candle snuffers, egg bowls, and spice boxes. Among the 'irons' were two iron-wheel spits with large 'cookholds', and balance-skewers, a pig iron and oven raker, steak tongs, and a wood-wheel spit. There were grid-irons for grilling, and trivets for standing cooking vessels over the fire. Cleavers were for chopping meat carcasses, and there were also meat saws, suet choppers, beef forks, and steak beaters.

The salting room was an important place. Stout square wooden salting-troughs, lined with lead, stood on legs there alongside solid wooden tables and forms, a chopping-block, meat-baskets, long-handled meat hooks, and four wire meat crowns. A six-foot kneading-trough was in the bakehouse, near two tall flour bins with flap tops. There too were a long wainscot table, a pail, an iron peel (a shovel used for taking loaves and pies in and out of the bread-oven), a scraper, and a scuffler.

Laundering was done in the wash-house in three large tubs which the laundry maid stirred with a stick called a dolly. From there the steaming wet sheets and clothes, after resting on a broad draining tray, went on their way to the laundry at the far end of the service wing. This was fitted with an array of ironing tables, mangles, wicker clothes-baskets, and airing horses. There were ten flat irons as well as iron stands, and a range of special-purpose irons – Italian irons, egg irons, and goffering irons for waving and crimping lace edges and fluted trimmings. The nearby dairy also had its specialist equipment: an upright barrel-shaped churn and staff, a large cheese tub with its cover, two wooden milking-cans, seven brown milk pans, and a supply of bowls, butter tubs and scales, cheese boards, and cheese vats.

The Cellar Book

Like most great houses at this time, Attingham had a busy brew-house and a well stocked cellar. A giant cellar book lists fifteen or more kinds of wines and spirits, and the butler's neat weekly totals show how many bottles were used and how many left in stock. Unfortunately it is less clear where the Berwicks bought their wine, though a notice of a wine auction at the *Fox Inn,* Shrewsbury, in 1814 has prices carefully jotted down against the various wines which were being offered for sale, and suggests that a lot may have been bought there.

Bottles were arranged in four groups and the contents of Cellars A, B, D, and E were checked separately. In 1808 – to take an average year – the cellars held some three hundred and fifty bottles of port, four hundred of sherry, a hundred and forty of madeira, fifty or so of brandy, twenty-seven of white brandy, and over thirty of champagne. There was also a good supply of claret and burgundy, as well as oddments of hock, malmsey, and rum.

A well-run house always had someone keeping a careful eye on outgoings from the cellar, and the record of ten days at Attingham in 1812 opens the cellar door and gives a cheering glimpse of one side of life there. On 9 February Lord and Lady Berwick arrived at the house, and the following day they sent a bottle of port and one of madeira to the steward's room. On 11 February the maids were given a bottle of port and on 12 February another went to the cook, who also had a bottle of sherry on 13 February. On the next two days three bottles of port and sherry were given to Shrewsbury tradesmen. On 17 February the cook had another bottle each of port and sherry, and so did the steward's room on 19 February. What is not quite clear is whether this wine was to be enjoyed by the staff with their meals, or to be used in the cooking.

The Berwicks certainly often gave wine to their servants. On Lady Berwick's birthday in 1812 three bottles each of port and sherry went to the steward's room, though oddly enough he had only half as many on Lord Berwick's birthday. When they arrived at Attingham after being away they often gave the cook a bottle of sherry and one of brandy, with two of each to the housekeeper and the other servants. And when they set off for London on a cold November day that year, they took a bottle of madeira and one of red hermitage with them in the carriage.

Both brew-house and beer cellars were busy places which called for a lot of specialist equipment. They held an array of iron-bound mash tuns, the largest a seven-footer. Alongside were beer stands, wooden chutes, and a square wicker hop-strainer. There was a massive two-hundred-and-forty-gallon cask, at least two eighty-gallon ones, and two eighty-gallon hogsheads. Smaller tools of the trade included an iron-bound funnel, tunpails, piggins (two-handled wooden bowls), mashing oars (for mixing malt with hot water before it was fermented), a tin skimmer, a hop sieve and ladder, tilts, and four rakers.

Some idea of what went on in the Attingham brew-house can be conjured up by a visit to Charlecote, in Warwickshire, where all the brewing equipment can still be seen and the various processes are clearly explained. In 1845, more than four thousand gallons of beer and ale were standing in the cellars there. Barley was grown on the estate, and was then taken to the malt-house in the village to be made into malt before being ground and carted to the brew-house. There it was brewed, and the beer was left in the fermenting tun for a day or so, to allow time for the yeast to begin to work. Then the beer was tunned – ladled into casks, which were stowed away in cellars under the house till it was ready to drink.

The Attingham inventory does not mention a copper boiler like the one that can still be seen at Charlecote. This held 240 gallons, and in it the water was brought to the boil and then allowed to cool. When it reached a temperature of 165° Fahrenheit, it was run from the copper boiler into a great 480-gallon mash tun, where grist (ground malted barley) was stirred into it with a mashing oar. When the grist was well mixed in, the mixture was left to stand for two or three hours while a sweet liquid known as wort was being formed. The wort was run off from the mash tun and pumped into a copper vessel above it. From there it dropped through a wooden trough into a strainer, standing in a long rectangular wooden vessel known as a cooler, where the spent hops were strained from the wort. After passage through a second cooler had reduced the temperature of the wort to about 65° Fahrenheit, it was run into a collecting and fermenting tun. At one time, cooling depended on the freshness of the atmosphere and so only took place during the winter months.

Tradesmen's Bills

During the last century most tradesmen were also craftsmen. In 1808 the second Lord Berwick did much of his shopping in Shrewsbury, already a thriving county town which drew countrypeople – as it still does – from both Wales and England to its market, shops, and, inns. Lord Berwick ran up bills with a number of retailers, many of whose names are unfamiliar today. Among them were the plasterer, druggist, cutler, hatter, whitesmith (who worked in tin and metal goods), netmaker, carrier, cheesemonger and cheese factor, brazier (worker in brass), glazier, perfumer, rope-maker, breeches-maker, pump-maker, china man, and wire worker. There should also be a map maker in the list, as Lord Berwick's bills included one for £141 – a large sum then – 'For Mapping Your Lordship's Estates'.

Sometimes one man followed several different trades. In 1818 a Shrewsbury 'Tin-Plate Worker, Brazier and Pewterer' supplied Attingham with hair sieves, brooms, brushes, mop-heads, a tinder-box with flints and steel, a pair of bellows, a corkscrew, two pairs of polished candle-snuffers, two water-cans and covers, and a painted chamber-pail with a cover. A great country house needed endless different kinds of brushes and brooms. There were banister brushes and 'cow mouth scouring brushes', black lead brushes and corner brushes, stair-carpet brushes, round table brushes and grate brushes, not to mention hair brooms, and carpet whisks. The tin-plate worker also made himself useful by tinning and repairing copper pots and pans, mending dripping-pans, and making new silk bottoms for worn sieves.

A bill without a heading, dated 1824, lists a supply of peppermint lozenges, bleaching liquid, Epsom salts, a case of indelible ink, tooth powder, white wax, salt lemons, saffron, extract of lead, Turkey rhubarb, gamboge (used as a purgative), and a bottle of hartshorn (made from the horns of deer and used as smelling-salts). There is also a bill for threepence for half an inch of logwood.

The doctor sent in his bill for visits to the house, and for medical supplies he brought with him. One year's account included a call to bleed one of the servants, a spasm mixture for Lady Berwick, a 'Lotion for Gnat Bites', and charges for powders, a box of pills, ointments, draughts (doses of liquid medicine), corn plasters, a 'plaister on thick leather', and tinctures (medicines made from the solution of vegetable elements in alcohol).

Thomas Groome, the tailor, did some useful mending jobs on servants' livery. He put new straps on the postilion's breeches and let out his and the coachman's coats. He mended the butler's breeches, repaired coats and waistcoats, and replaced worn pockets.

Richard Partridge, Lord Berwick's steward, kept methodical accounts. In 1812 his purchases included fresh river and sea fish, as well as live tame birds and animals. Twelve pounds of turbot cost sixteen shillings, lobsters were two shillings a pound, four pounds of eels came to three shillings and fourpence, and salmon varied in price from one and threepence a pound in August 1812 to three and sixpence for Severn salmon a year later. A singing thrush cost one pound five shillings, and other purchases included two cages of ducks, two pans of fish, canaries, bullfinches, geese, and tame rabbits. Frequent payments were made to local people who came to work at the Park: to cut wood and make faggots (bundles of sticks tied together for fuel), to catch rats, to bake and to brew, to weed, and to clean the stableyard and the flags in the courtyard.

Other expenses were less humdrum. Lady Berwick had a bill from her harp master which included his fee for a concert. In 1846 over six pounds was spent on groceries and other supplies from Fortnum and Mason in Piccadilly, and a few days later an eighteen-month-old Cheshire cheese, costing nearly two pounds, was a toothsome addition to the larder.

The Gardens and Stables

At the start of the nineteenth century the Attingham gardeners were busily at work in the fine park, which had recently been landscaped by Repton to frame the River Tern as it wanders on the last lap of its way to the Severn.

The garden accounts list many things that are still needed and used today. A peck of early potatoes was both cheap and early at 1s 6d in

Scenes of domestic employment by W. H. Pyne (early nineteenth century).
(Above: gardening; below: dairying)

February. Other purchases were a pair of garden shears, a pruning saw, a chisel, a pound of powder for three shillings, four pounds of shot for one shilling, two hundred nails for repairing the garden fence, and two pounds of tobacco and four of sulphur 'for the trees'. Casual labour was taken on for digging at sixpence a rood, four shillings were paid for eight journeys to Shrewsbury to fetch tar, and another four shillings went on two days' work mending garden barrows. Vegetable seed was surprisingly expensive in the early years of the last century: an ounce of 'collyflower' seed cost two shillings and sixpence (more than a day's wages for a labourer), endive seed cost eightpence an ounce, while the same amount of green 'coss' lettuce seed came to a shilling.

Already in February men were at work in the hothouse. As well as their wages, entries include tobacco 'for the use of the hothouse'. The men who worked there during the sultry days of June must have welcomed their allowance of £1 5s worth of ale. And it was not only in summer that men doing heavy work had extra rations of food and drink; a generous supply of beer and meat was allowed in March for workmen who were filling the ice-house.

Skilled specialists needed on the estate included the local leather-craftsman, who was kept busy with work for the coachman, the stables, and the keeper. New straps, head collars, buckles, and billets (small metal bars) were needed by the coachman, who also had a broken bridle to be mended. The keeper needed a 'very strong dog chain', two pairs of couples (to link dogs together), a new dog whip, and six brass jointed dog-collars. But the leather-craftsman's main work was for the stables: finely made goods bought for their use included six halters, a new rein with plate and buckle, a horse brush and curry comb, a Pelham bridle, a silk whip cord, and two straps each for Lord Berwick's boots and gaiters. It was helpful that the leather-craftsman did not consider odd jobs of mending harness and saddles beneath him. On at least one occasion he even did a welcome repair to the mangle straps in the laundry.

By the 1820s, when the second Lord Berwick was still spending lavishly on his gardens and park, there was endless outside work to be done. Men were paid for loading bark and grinding barley, for carrying thorns, and for moving larch trees from the copse. Parcels and hampers were always arriving at Attingham from London, and among local deliveries that called for careful handling were a supply of

181

pheasants' eggs and – a good five shillings' worth – a basket of peacocks.

On the King's Highway

The second Lord Berwick was often away from home – in Italy as well as in London and elsewhere. Though the family travelled in their own carriages, parcels and lesser travellers went by the coaches that linked all parts of the country, and the Attingham papers include some interesting coaching bills from the pre-railway years.

Coaches provided an efficient shuttle service from town to town, and brought thirsty travellers, baggage, and tired horses to the coaching-inns which were their rallying-points. The services they offered were advertised on bills with printed headings. A link with the Continent was offered by William Horne at the *Golden Cross*, Charing Cross. From there, he proclaimed, 'passengers and parcels are conveyed by mail, telegraph, and other coaches to the principal seaports, cities, commercial towns, and most fashionable watering-places in the Kingdom, also PARIS DILIGENCES Morning and Evening, by which passengers and parcels are forwarded to all parts of the Continent, and are the only conveyances connected with the Messageries Royales, Rue notre Dame des Victoires, Paris'.

Other coaches used by the Attingham household were based on the *Swan with Two Necks*, Lad-Lane, and on *The George and Blue Boar*, Holborn. Brown's Gloucester Warehouse, on the corner of Oxford Street and Park Street, was an important starting-point for coaches heading for all parts of England, Ireland, Scotland, and Wales. From there horses and carts could also be rented, and it was proudly claimed that coaches travelled to, and through, Oxford nine times every day, and that parcels booked in before midday went off by the mail to any part of the kingdom that same evening.

The transport industry in the early years of the nineteenth century was efficient and adaptable. A hamper of spa water was sent to London for 9s 6d. Two cages of ducks and two pans of fish came from there to Attingham by wagon, not by coach, and must have had a much slower journey. Three guineas were paid as guard's allowance on the carriage of a letter-bag, and when Lord Berwick hired horses for a journey to his home in 1813 he paid two guineas for eight post-horses. They travelled seven miles at six shillings a mile and he also paid ten shillings for the ostler and the post-boys who came with them.

In 1821 it cost twelve guineas to send four horses, with stable boys to look after them, to Epsom races. Payments for turnpikes and ostlers as the family carriage bowled along the road from London to Attingham cost over four pounds, but 'posting' was much more expensive. This was express travelling, when relays of fresh horses were hired to gallop from stage to stage at top speed, and the cost of doing this from London to Attingham with three pairs of horses came to £48.

Turnpike charges varied according to the different vehicles which were passing through. At one point on the road 4s 3d was paid for the phaeton (a light open four-wheeled carriage, usually drawn by a pair of horses), 2s 3d for the chariot (a four-wheeler with back seats only), 1s 6d for the dog-cart (a two-wheeled driving-cart with cross seats back to back, so-called because originally there was a compartment for dogs), while 2s 3d was the charge for the saddle horses. For a family who lived as far from London as the Berwicks, horses and carriages were an important part of the establishment. No wonder the blacksmith's bill for a year came to over £100.

10

Chatsworth House

THE CAVENDISHES
and their house in Derbyshire

Chatsworth was bought for £600 in 1549 by Sir William Cavendish, and he and his wealthy and ambitious third wife, Elizabeth, best known as Bess of Hardwick, set to work to build a house on the left bank of the river Derwent. After her husband's death in 1557, Bess completed the great square Tudor house in which Mary Queen of Scots is said to have been more than once a prisoner. The main core of Bess's house was even larger than the Chatsworth of today, and it stood intact for over a hundred years.

The fourth Earl of Devonshire, later the first Duke, had no intention of pulling down all of Bess's Chatsworth when he inherited it in 1684. But in fact that was precisely what he did, rebuilding the house front by front, almost room by room. When he died, in 1707, his great baroque palace, with its noble classical façades, had little but its site in common with what had been there before. But such a haphazard way of building, without any organic master-plan, produced a house that was very awkward to live in, and the fourth Duke's improvements during the second half of the eighteenth century aimed at remedying this. He added a new entrance court, which had on its east side a low range of service buildings – stable, wash-house, dairy, bakehouse, and kitchen.

During the nineteenth century, Chatsworth was just one of many homes belonging to the four Dukes and their three families . (The sixth Duke of Devonshire lived and died a bachelor.) Vast and splendid in its magnificent park, for long weeks it lay empty, silent, and unlit, as the Devonshires were often away. They travelled, stayed with their friends, and visited their homes elsewhere. By the middle of the century these included Lismore Castle in Ireland, Compton Place in Sussex, Bolton Abbey in Yorkshire, Holker Hall in Lancashire, Hardwick, just a few miles away over the moors, and their two London homes, Devonshire House in Piccadilly, and Chiswick House in the nearby village on the Thames.

Whether the family were at home or not, the house and grounds were open daily from ten to five, and visitors were shown the rooms, the gardens, and the famous waterworks. By the middle of the century there were, according to Leigh Hunt, some forty-eight thousand visitors each year. Joseph Paxton, the sixth Duke's gardener and friend, put the figure at sixty thousand when he was campaigning for the new railway; he was probably right as it was his wife Sarah who showed many of the visitors around. The railway came at last in 1849, and the number of visitors had grown to eighty-four thousand by the end of the 1890s.

Farington tells of life at the beginning of the century. In 1801 an elderly villager told him that the Duke lived in great style. Sometimes as many as a hundred and eighty guests, with their servants, were put up at the house. Visitors' horses were stabled in the Chatsworth stalls until these – there were some eighty of them – were full. When there was no more room in the stables, the horses were cared for at the inn in the village.

The sixth Duke succeeded a few months after his coming-of-age party in 1811. This was a great occasion, for which a thousand pairs of knives and forks as well as twenty carvers were bought. But the house he inherited was dreadfully uncomfortable and inconvenient, and he set to work on an ambitious programme of new building and rearranging, with Jeffry Wyatt – he later changed his name to Wyatville – in command of operations. One of the sixth Duke's welcome improvements was the new coach-house he provided for the many carriages which trundled his guests over the hilly Derbyshire roads, down through Capability Brown's tree-dotted park, and across the bridge over the Derwent. Charles Greville described an 'immense party' given by the Duke in November, 1829, when forty people sat down to dinner every day and there were about a hundred and fifty servants in the steward's room and servants' hall. 'All the resources of the house – horses, carriages, keepers, etc. – are placed at the disposal of the guests, and everybody does what they like best.' It is interesting to compare Greville's impressions on this occasion with those of a later visit he paid to Chatsworth. In October 1843 he wrote,

Chatsworth is very magnificent, but I looked back with regret to the house in its unfinished state... The comfort we had then has been ill exchanged for the magnificence which has replaced it, and he has made the House so large that he can't afford to live in it, and never remains there above two or three months in the year.

As usual the stables were a separate department, with their own staff and accounts. As well as run-of-the-mill supplies of oats and hay, there were buckets and besoms (brooms made of twigs tied round a stick-handle), saddling, harness repairs, coach-making, and shoeing to be accounted for. Payments were made for post-horses, and other horses were bought, hired and sometimes transported (later by train). Medicine for horses was quite a big item, as was baiting (feeding horses on a journey). One entry in the accounts is for the painting of horses' names on their stalls. A clue to the importance of the stables is that in 1875, to take a year at random, their cost came to £271, roughly a fifteenth of the total outlay of £4,237 on Chatsworth.

Records of the sixth Duke's early years as master of Chatsworth tell mainly of utilitarian jobs that were done on the estate. Palisades were made, wooden piles in the river bank were tipped with iron shoes, the bank itself was shored up with timber, and sand left by floods was carted away. Women and boys had the jobs of clearing rubbish from the park and spreading molehills. The fish-ponds were repaired, and fishing-cloths and cast-nets were bought. Otter-hunting on the river was a popular local sport; the cost of some otterhound whelps is entered in the accounts alongside the waterkeeper's wages.

Other outdoor jobs were shifting gateposts, cleaning the rookery, reframing wheelbarrows, and making and putting up new floodgates in the park. As well as plentiful game there was a herd of deer at Chatsworth, and teams of farm-horses brought loads of hay and beans as fodder for them. Some of the work was for specialists – carpenters, smiths, sawyers, plumbers, glaziers, plasterers, and farriers. Walls had to be built and repaired, roads made, gates painted, tools mended and sharpened, trees and hedges planted and protected – by palings – from the deer. There were also jobs which could be done by casual labour from the village and nearby farms. Frightening birds, threshing and cutting oats and wheat, hay-making, hedging, and removing earth and ashes had to be done carefully, but they were all unskilled jobs.

When the new building operations got under way an army of men were on the Chatsworth pay-list. By 1821 there were ninety-two masons, forty-six labourers and forty-five quarrymen. Less than a year later, when the north wing was begun, a hundred and sixty masons and seventy-four labourers were at work. The clerk of the works was paid £3 a week, a joiner got five shillings, five carpenters and four sawyers got 3s 6d each, and masons' pay varied from 1s 8d to 3s 8d.

Staff Quarters

Before Wyatt and the sixth Duke began reorganizing and adding to Chatsworth it was a very awkward house to live or work in. For one thing, the main entrance was through the present north courtyard which had on its west side a derelict shrubbery, used as a rubbish dump, and on the other the staff working rooms. So even the most eminent visitors had to pass stables, poultry coops, wash-house, dairy, scullery, bakehouse, kitchens, pastry room, and larder before reaching the front door. Each department had its occupational smell – many of them not at all pleasant or appetizing.

Even when they were inside the front door, trials lay ahead for visitors. They still had to go past squalid staff quarters (including the cook's bedroom and the back stairs) before they reached the great hall. Years later, in the *Handbook* he printed privately in 1844, the sixth Duke described for his sister the many improvements that had been made since they were children at Chatsworth together. In the early years of the century the further side of the entrance courtyard had been, he reminded her, an 'impervious wood' where the cooks dumped their refuse. When the children ventured into it they came across 'meat-safes, and larders, and carpenters' pits, and dog-kennels and dark recesses for lumber'. When Wyatt was commissioned in 1817 to plan big alterations, these included a new wing, to house kitchens and other offices, where the old working quarters had been. An odd side-effect of the old kitchen's central position, in what later became the entrance hall, was the small window above the kitchen, through which the family and their guests could look down from the gallery above and watch the cooks at work on their next meal.

The house was very antiquated before the Duke and Wyatt set to work. It was also alarmingly inflammable. On one occasion the wooden stairs at the back of what was called the tea-room – it served as a still-room or housekeeper's store-room – caught fire. The fifth Duke's French confectioner, Monsieur Caille, panicked when he saw flames through the cracks between the floor-boards, and he had the unlucky idea of emptying on them the kettle he was carrying. But the kettle contained melted sugar, so he merely fed the flames with caramel.

The staff quarters were a strange mixture of splendour and squalor. A fine Elizabethan alabaster panel representing Apollo and the Muses

A butler at Chatsworth

A Cellarman at Chatsworth by
W. Baker

lay unnoticed in the steward's room until the Duke moved it to more fitting surroundings in the old library at Hardwick. Yet the large nursery where Selina Trimmer, the governess, presided was a 'smoky old place', and looked out on the blackened backs of some sculptured busts in the courtyard below.

Before the alterations, most of the ground-floor rooms had been occupied by servants. The cook and the housekeeper had bedrooms there, though others had to reach theirs by way of a dark ladder of a staircase, known as the four-score-and-four. Wyatt and the Duke made living conditions much better for the staff, giving the housekeeper three ground-floor rooms where the tea-room and footmen's room had been before. The new kitchen was handsome and roomy, fitted with steam cupboards and a hot steam table. These were heated by coke and, when wood was the only fuel used in the huge grate, the place became much less smoky. Even so, staff quarters were still far from perfect. The Duke told his sister that the pastry – as they called the room where pies and tarts were made – was convenient now, but the scullery was awful, and the larder atrocious as 'it looks into the abysses of a dusty coal-yard'.

Good and Bad Servants

Whether the family were away or at home, the servants were expected to take the initiative in getting things done. The sixth Duke's *Handbook* recalls how his father was asleep one night in his bedroom when he was woken with the news that the house was on fire. The story goes that he merely 'turned round to sleep on his other side, observing that they had better try to put it out'.

The sixth Duke felt that his cook, Mr Howard, ought to be the best in the world. He had been with him a long time and when he was in Paris the Duke had asked Louis XVIII to place him in his kitchen. The King agreed, and Mr Howard worked there for several months and also trained in two famous restaurants. Not all great houses had an upholsterer on the staff, as Chatsworth did throughout the nineteenth century. John Crace did great things during the Duke's refurbishings, and his employer said that he transformed the lower library, 'making it look something between an illuminated manuscript and a café in the rue de Richelieu'.

A bachelor master, uninterested in household details and often away from home, provided plenty of opportunities for below-stairs skulduggery. On one occasion the family lawyer was in despair because he could not persuade the Duke to take any action about a 'monstrous wine bill'. Another time an attendant helped himself to £500 of the housekeeping money, and spent it on gambling. And one of the valets de chambre had bad luck at the Doncaster races, borrowed his master's gun, and shot himself in his room.

At one time the Duke had a courier called Kuhlbach, who travelled with him on the Continent. He was a lurid character, accused of keeping a houseful of prostitutes and of debauching his own daughter when she was only just out of school in Paris. Then there was a steward who narrowly avoided being arrested for debt; and a body-servant, Meynell, who was always getting drunk, was finally dismissed after being discovered in a brothel. The tolerant Duke was willing to put up with his servants' failings, but Meynell went too far when the Duke's own dog was found in the brothel too. Even so, the man was given a generous pension.

For years the Chatsworth housekeeper was Hannah Gregory, the aunt of Sarah Bown, who married Joseph Paxton. Mrs Gregory had been there all her life and was still housekeeper, though no longer able to do the job, when she died in 1843 aged seventy-seven. Mrs Paxton's sister, Mary, had learned the work from her aunt and was ready to take it on, but the Duke had his own ideas. He offered the post to a Miss Bicknell who worked at a local inn. It was a disastrous appointment. The new housekeeper began ordering flowers and fruit for her friends, took them to Hardwick with Chatsworth staff to wait on them, and finally gave a musical party in the Duke's private rooms. That was a fatal slip. Although the public were allowed to see the house, certain rooms were more private than others, and entry tickets were of several colours each admitting visitors to different parts of the house. The Duke abhorred the thought of strangers in his own apartments, so Miss Bicknell's term of office was as short as it was inglorious.

Twenty years later, in the seventh Duke's time, one of his daughters-in-law had great difficulties in choosing and managing her maids. Lady Frederick Cavendish wrote a diary, which is still entertaining and touching to read. She was a religious lady who turned – often in vain, it must be admitted – to prayer and the Bible for help with her staff problems. These were specially tricky when she took her maid with her to stay at Chatsworth. 'I am worried', she wrote in 1866, 'by my new maid turning out dreadfully huffy with the Duke's household, and unmanageable when I tell her to show my gowns to other people. She is going.' She had been unlucky with maid after maid, and this was the fourth who had behaved badly to other servants. 'It perplexes me sadly how all I say and do, though it is not without prayer, seems to fail utterly,' she wrote. It was all because of petty jealousy and pride. Servants had their own code of morals, and Lady Frederick noticed that this included two paramount commandments: 'Thou shalt never let thyself be put upon; and thou shalt attribute the meanest motive to the conduct of thy fellows.'

It was only her personal maids who were too much for Lady Frederick. She enjoyed a servants' ball in the Chatsworth banqueting room shortly before Christmas, though a few days earlier she had been 'shivering all over with a miserable scene with my maid who squabbles with all the servants'. But deliverance was at hand. That same week there is a more cheerful entry in the diary: 'To my inexpressible relief and comfort, my odious little maid went off, and gentle, pleasant-looking, quiet little Mrs Parry came, who will probably turn out a Felon, but is meanwhile very soothing.' Poor Lady Frederick, and poor Mrs Parry! Felony was not their only problem. A few days after starting her new job Mrs Parry discovered that she 'was several months gone with a luckless baby!' Lady Frederick hoped 'to manage a stop-gap, and take the poor thing back'. But the diary never tells whether she did, or what became of the luckless baby.

No Ordinary Gardener

Without any doubt, the person who did most for Chatsworth in the nineteenth century was the genius whom the sixth Duke had the wisdom to spot and appoint, when Paxton was only twenty-three, as his gardener. The Chatsworth gardens were nothing much before then. The Duke's *Handbook* records that 'Paxton found four pine-houses, bad; two vineries, containing eight bunches of grapes; two good peach-houses and a few cucumber frames.' There were no glasshouses for plants, no vegetables, and no new plants had been added since about 1800. But the Duke had, as he put it, 'got bit by gardening'. His favourite home at Chiswick was next door to the grounds of the Royal Horticultural Society, where he used to enjoy walking. The young man who was a gardener there would open the gate for him, they would walk together, and the Duke was struck by his exceptional intelligence. So he suggested that Paxton should give up his job at Chiswick, where he was earning twenty-three shillings a week, and come to Chatsworth as head gardener. It was a risk for both, and one of the most important decisions they ever made. The head of the Chiswick gardens could say no more about Paxton than that he was 'young and untried', and the Duke was to sail for Russia (to attend the coronation of Czar Nicholas I) two days later.

Paxton has left his own description of how he started his new job:

> I left London by the Comet coach for Chesterfield arrived at Chatsworth at half past four o'clock in the morning of the ninth of May, 1826. As no person was to be seen at that early hour, I got over the greenhouse gate by the old covered way, explored the pleasure-grounds, and looked round the outside of the house. I then went down to the kitchen-gardens, scaled the outside wall, and saw the whole of the place. Set the men to work there at six o'clock: then returned to Chatsworth, and got Thomas Weldon to play me the water-works, and afterwards went to breakfast with poor dear Mrs Gregory and her niece. The latter fell in love with me, and I with her, and this completed my first morning's work at Chatsworth before nine o'clock.

At that pace, things began to move. The Duke later recalled how quickly Paxton transformed the Chatsworth gardens. Vegetables, fruit, and flowers in perfection began to appear, and gardeners and labourers were set to work. The old greenhouse was heated, and a new one, and three orchid houses, were built. To make his arboretum Paxton cleared and thinned a site where previously trees had been grown for timber. Eventually two thousand species were planted, and a walk nearly a mile long was made. For his first year's work Paxton was paid £70.

It is interesting to see how soon the Duke began consulting Paxton about his other affairs. In 1829 the young man was made forester as well as head gardener, and a few years later he took charge of road-building too. Smithers, the Chatsworth agent, and Ridgeway, the house steward, found that he was soon taking over their duties as well. In 1834 the Duke was in London and he asked Paxton to come up and

A portrait of Joseph Paxton, the sixth Duke of Devonshire's gardener, by
H. P. Briggs

settle some business with his lawyer there. There were plans afoot for 'the Great Stove', as the famous conservatory was called. 'It is clear that I must have some home for my plants,' the Duke wrote to Paxton, 'but I am glad you agree with me as to this £26,000 being too much to lay out.' Paxton certainly did agree. He could envisage large-scale costly schemes, but he still took care of his employer's pennies. 'I shall never like to pay 2s 6d for growing a pound of grapes when I could have grown them for 1s,' he said. Five years after his arrival at Chatsworth, he had twenty-two men working on twelve acres of kitchen garden, and there were thirty hothouses and pits. Paxton heated his houses by fire flues rather than hot water, and he preferred wood structures to metal because they cost £500 instead of £1,800.

The Duke and Paxton were pioneers in the enterprise of fetching exotic plants and trees from far countries. In 1834 the Duke was in Paris, collecting seeds and plants, when he sent word to Paxton to join him there as soon as possible. He showed him personally the sights of Paris – the Palais Royal, the Luxembourg Palace and Gardens, the Jardin des Plantes, the Père-Lachaise Cemetery, and the Tuileries. Paxton also saw the fountains at Versailles. Back in England again, the Duke and his gardener went off on another tour, visiting estates and gardens at Dropmore, Windsor, Woburn, Wilton, Fonthill, and elsewhere, collecting and exchanging ideas. In 1838 they set off on a year of travelling – from Geneva to Italy, Malta, Greece, and Constantinople.

It is impossible to cover all Paxton's achievements in a short chapter. In 1829 he brought along a Douglas pine sapling, small enough to be carried in his hat, and between then and 1845 he watched it grow to a height of thirty-five feet. In 1830 all his ingenuity was needed to move a large weeping ash from near Derby, so that it could be planted in the Chatsworth courtyard, where it still stands. Another time the finest trees from the Tankerville collection had to be brought to Derbyshire. This meant pulling down the house they were in and then rebuilding it, inventing and making special carriages, and demolishing and replacing turnpike gates so that the giant load could get by.

Probably the most famous of Paxton's achievements at Chatsworth was the Great Stove for tropical plants, which was begun in 1836, and finished and planted in 1840. The largest glass building in the world, it was two hundred and seventy-seven feet long, a hundred and twenty-three feet broad, and sixty-seven feet at its highest point. Paxton designed it with central and side aisles wide enough for the Duke to drive through it in a carriage and pair. By a characteristically ingenious 'contrivance', the Stove was heated by underground furnaces which were fed with coal by a railway, so that the Duke proudly claimed that it was 'the only hothouse known, to remain in which longer than ten minutes does not produce a state of suffering'. The Great Stove cost £10,000 to build, and £2,000 a year to run. Another original and effective invention of Paxton's was the 'conservative wall', warmed by flues, and protected in winter by curtains, which provided shelter for tender plants along a walk between the house and the stables. Then there were the great rock garden, the waterfall, the Victoria Regia lily house, the Emperor lake, and the fountain, at nearly three hundred feet the highest gravity-fed fountain in the world. To make a reservoir to feed it through nearly four miles of pipes, over a hundred thousand cubic yards of soil had to be shifted. As if this were not enough, the village of Edensor was rebuilt, on model village lines, further away from the big house.

Paxton's life story has been told elsewhere. This account is concerned only with the work he did for the Duke, and the remarkable relationship between them. Already in 1836 the Duke valued his young gardener highly enough to commission his portrait from a painter who charged what was then the steep price of £60. And the ups and downs of travelling together seem not to have upset the *entente*. 'Very happy and comfortable with Paxton,' the Duke noted in his diary. And in spite of occasional grumbles that Paxton sometimes slept and ruminated when he would like to talk, he was quick to allow that 'he is everything for me'. He did not find it difficult to express his feelings to Paxton. 'I had rather all the flowers in the garden were dead than you ill,' he once wrote to him.

There was nothing one-sided about their relationship. Paxton's first loyalty was always to the Duke and to Chatsworth, even after fame, and eventually a knighthood, had come to him through his work, his journalism, his business successes, his championship of the railway, his famous design for the 1851 Crystal Palace, and his years as a Member of Parliament. In 1838 he could have had the job of looking after the royal gardens at Windsor at a yearly salary of £1,000. But he did not even consider accepting the offer. 'I am sure the Duke would be miserable,' he explained to his wife, 'and very justly think me ungrateful.' Eventually Paxton sat down to meals with the Duke, but Sarah had the tact not to expect to join them. It was only when the Duke died that Paxton's life-work at Chatsworth came to an end. Deeply grieved, he wrote at once to his successor, resigning after thirty-two years of active and devoted service.

Of course Chatsworth had other gardeners. Before Paxton's time the Duke remembered John Barton in his blue apron; he used to make small hand-fishing nets for him and his sister. Barton served under Mr Travis, less popular with the children, and easy to visualize from the Duke's description. He was, he said, 'prolix, old school, and very consequential, in a cocked hat and striped stockings, and gold shoe-buckles, wearing powder and a long pigtail'. By Paxton's time such colourful old characters had given place to a new race of gardeners. In 1835 young John Gibson, after only two years in the Chatsworth gardens, was sent on a plant-collecting trip to India. That year, a second expedition ended in tragedy when two other young gardeners went on a journey to California and were drowned. Both were paid twenty-four shillings a week, whether they were working in England or travelling, and it is interesting to learn that one of the two spoke French fluently while the other was a good Latin scholar. It was not only the head gardener who was a man of parts.

The Duke's 'Contrivances'

Chatsworth was a great place for what the sixth Duke called his 'contrivances'. One of these was a jack, turned by water, which was to be found in a courtyard on the way to the kitchen. Not far away was a device for preserving fish alive in water 'till the moment of execution'. And the Duke explained to his sister how his new arrangements provided three baths, with water for the largest of them 'heated by retorts over the fire in a vault underneath'. From there a slanting pipe brought the water to the coiled pipes which filled the whole space under the perforated tiles of the floor. These circulated the water and cooled it to the right temperature so that there was no steam in the bathroom.

Heating the vast house was a formidable problem. After the 'improvements' the library was warmed by 'Price's apparatus', which was fixed partly in the cellar under the leather-room, and partly under the west corridor. The heat was regulated by valves placed at the top and bottom of a bookcase, while an 'air-drain' in the west front of the house allowed for ventilation. The same machinery warmed the west sub-hall, the chapel, and the western end of the north corridor.

Beer was brewed above the stables. By another ingenious 'contrivance' it was carried from there to what the Duke described as the 'endless labyrinth' of the beer cellars, through a three-inch underground pipe, over a thousand feet long. The Duke told his sister that the thought of that pipe with its stream of newly-brewed beer always gave him 'a longing, on some great occasion, to form a fountain of that liquid'. The account books tell of money spent on hops, on buying and grinding malt, on assistants for the brewing, and on repairs to the beer-pipes. In one fortnight in September 1848, more than three hundred and fifty gallons of ale and a thousand gallons of beer were drawn. That gives some idea of the scale on which Chatsworth brewing was done.

But what was up-to-date in the 1840s looked very old-fashioned by the end of the century. Gradually, new inventions and manufactures arrived. In 1893 water turbines were introduced, and Chatsworth was one of the first great houses to have electric light. A few years later, all the washing for the Devonshire establishments in Piccadilly, Chiswick, Hardwick, and Bolton was done in the Chatsworth laundry, which was the proud possessor of a steel boiler. This heated a steel table in the kitchen, a drying rack in the brushing-room, and a hot cupboard near the big dining-room. All the machinery was driven by water-power from the lake high up on the moors above the house, and this also supplied the turbines for the electricity and the Emperor fountain.

State Occasions

Even if the fountains were never made to run with beer, great occasions at Chatsworth were splendid affairs. In 1832, when she was thirteen, Princess Victoria came on a visit with her mother, the Duchess of Kent. It was the Princess's first dinner party, and the household staff made sure that everything went smoothly, by having what the Duke called a 'cooked rehearsal' the day before. It was also a first occasion for the great dining-room, which had just been splendidly rearranged, decorated, and upholstered. The Devonshire gold plate which the Duke had taken with him to Russia was safely home again and gleamed on the table. The footmen were hardly less brilliant in the Cavendish livery of canary-yellow coats, blue breeches, and white stockings, with powdered wigs.

The Princess was impressed, and interested in everything. She inspected the kitchen and found it 'superb' in its size and cleanliness. Paxton stage-managed some magnificent outside effects. The famous water-works played non-stop throughout the visit; one night all the basins, cascades, and fountains were dazzlingly floodlit, with thousands of lights reflected in the water. An interesting detail did not escape the Princess's attention. Noticing how neat the gardens looked every morning, she discovered that Paxton employed a team of a hundred men to work through the night, clearing away fallen leaves and branches, sweeping paths, and rolling lawns. Paxton had been at Chatsworth only six years but he had already made his mark. An account in a local paper mentions that it was under his direction, as the Duke's forester, that trees were planted by the Princess and her mother to commemorate their visit.

Eleven years later, in 1843, Queen Victoria and Prince Albert made it known to the Duke that they would like to stay at Chatsworth. Paxton was in London at the time, so he wired to Sarah to engage a troop of casual labourers and to see that all the paths were freshly gravelled. The Duke met the royal party at Chesterfield station with a coach and six, and guns fired a salute from the Hunting Tower on the hill as they drew up at the house.

As well as the Queen and Prince Albert, the party included the Duke of Wellington, Lord Melbourne, and a large and distinguished retinue. The bedroom list tells how the guests were allotted to over thirty bedrooms. Two oxen, fifteen sheep, and four lambs were among the supplies that found their way to the kitchen. Police attendance cost the Duke £71 4s, and he paid £255 for the services of a military band, £69 for the hire of plate, and £103 19s for horses. The Queen wrote to her uncle, the King of the Belgians, that she was 'quite charmed and delighted' with everything at Chatsworth. It combined splendour and comfort, everything was beautifully done, and she noticed that many improvements had been made since her earlier visit.

Many other guests enjoyed the Duke's hospitality. In 1854 the King of Portugal came to luncheon, and a year later a large house party lasted a whole week. Over a hundred guests sat down to eat at the Duke's table, and meals were served in eight different rooms to the servants who came with them. Numbers fluctuated from day to day; there were sometimes as many as a hundred and eleven in the steward's room, and a hundred and twenty-two in the servants' hall. Forty-two ate in the kitchen, twenty-six in the scullery, seven in the confectionery, twenty-four in the pantry, and thirty-eight in the wash-house.

The seventh Duke was master of Chatsworth when the Prince and Princess of Wales stayed there in 1872. Lady Frederick Cavendish, the daughter-in-law whose failures with her maids have already been described, wrote in her diary about the intricate arrangements for the royal visit. On 14 December, three days before the Prince and Princess were due to arrive, preparations were already well under way. 'The house is getting into order,' she writes. 'All is being pondered and pre-arranged in true deliberate Cavendish style; and I quite expect that when once the whole machine is given a shove on Tuesday off it will go, everything in its proper place, from the Duke to the scullery-maid.'

Most of the guests – Lady Frederick calls them the '*avant-garde de la grande armée*' – arrived the day before the Prince and Princess, who were met off the royal train by the Duke and his eldest son. The two guests of honour took their breakfast quietly, *tête-à-tête*, in the red velvet room before joining a shooting-party in the park. A sumptuous luncheon was provided in the Russian cottage, but even Cavendish plans sometimes misfired, and on this occasion all the drinks were forgotten and had to be fetched, and sugar was served with the pie instead of salt. However, everything else went according to plan. Supper in the sculpture gallery was followed by floodlighting, water-works, and a county ball. The next day there was a 'mighty dinner' and another dance, this time only for those who were staying in the house as well as a few dinner-guests. Then came supper 'at various little tables in the big drawing-room, capitally managed'.

Paying the Bills

The new buildings and garden features at Chatsworth during the early nineteenth century cost vast sums. Running expenses were also huge, and the sixth Duke did not consider how his budget was to be balanced until he had to. Year after year more and more thousands of pounds were spent on Chatsworth. In 1820 the total was £6,420; by 1833 it was £197,251, without counting the architect's fees. In 1844, when Paxton had become his agent, the Duke's net income was £112,300 and – Micawber-like – his normal expenditure was £112,750. From this, £30,000 went on the house-steward's account, £10,250 on the gardens, and £4,500 on game, rates, and charities. Extra expenses between 1817 and 1843 included £269,689 on Chatsworth and £33,099 on the Great Stove. Nearly £200,000 was spent on furnishings, roads, and estate improvements at other houses besides Chatsworth. In 1856 the fuel bill for heating the house, the conservatory and hothouses came to £1,110. Paxton had made his plans without realizing that the Duke could not afford them. Now there were formidable debts to pay off. This was done by following Paxton's proposals to raise the money by selling Devonshire estates elsewhere.

The sixth Duke died in 1858, and his nephew lived much less extravagantly. The account books show that Chatsworth cost him £4,237 in 1875, £3,069 in 1876, £4,402 in 1877, and £3,338 ten years later, in 1887. Total figures give a blurred picture of living conditions, so it may be interesting to break down the money spent in one year. In 1875, for example, provisions came to £2,074, wages cost £316, furniture, repairs etc. accounted for £417, and £271 was spent on the stables. Peanuts – to use an un-Victorian word – compared with the gargantuan expenditure of the 1840s.

EPILOGUE

Today

So much for the past. Today the visitors pass through the state rooms, the sculpture galleries and libraries, up the marble stairs, and out to the gardens and the stables without so much as a thought for the everyday slog that kept the great houses in running order – for the stewards and housekeepers, the grooms of the chamber, the butlers, valets, footmen, maids, cooks, coachmen, and others who once lived and worked there. How many of the hundreds who stop to buy postcards and guidebooks in what was once a busy, clattering kitchen, or who sit down to tea where the housekeeper used to preside over a long staff table in the servants' hall, pause to remember the daily goings-on which the old rooms have witnessed?

Family portraits make it easier, perhaps, to imagine what happened upstairs: the duke and duchess with their children in the yellow drawing-room, the Chinese room, or the state saloon; or the marquess and marchioness with their guests in the long gallery, the chapel, or the armoury. But it is important to remember that the servants almost always outnumbered the family and their visitors, and that the man-hours spent in cooking, polishing, waiting, and on other day-to-day jobs added up to far more than those other hours which gently and quietly – though no less relentlessly – ticked away on the Tompion clock in the drawing-room whose windows looked out over the deer-park.

When the family were away the houses must have been cold, dark, and sad until their owners came back and breathed warmth and movement once again into the brilliant drawing-rooms, bedrooms, and halls. But even without their families, the houses were still alive. There could have been no life at all, no royal visits or state entertaining, no tenants' balls or daily meals, no bringing-up of children, or comings and goings in coaches and carriages, had it not been for all those unremembered men and women whose lives and work went on endlessly, year after year, below stairs.

Bibliography

Attingham Archives
Bedford Office Archives
The Devonshire MSS
Hatfield House Archives
Holkham Archives
The Pembroke Papers
Petworth House Archives

Adams, Samuel and Sarah, *The Complete Servant*, London, 1825
Albemarle, *see* Keppel
Anon., *The Art of Dining*, 1852
  The Footman's Guide, 1837
  Holkham Guidebooks, 1826, 1835, 1861
  The Servant's Guide and Family Manual, 1830
  The Servant's Practical Guide, Frederick Warne, 1880
Arbuthnot, Mrs Harriet, *Journal, 1820-32*, ed. Francis Bamford and the Duke of
  Wellington, Macmillan, 1950
Avery, Gillian, *Victorian People*, Collins, 1970
Bath, *see* Thynne
Beeton, Isabella, *The Book of Household Management*, London, 1861
Berry, Miss Mary, *Journals and Correspondence, 1783-1852*, ed. Lady Theresa Lewis,
  3 vols, Longmans, 1865
Blakiston, Georgiana, *Lord William Russell and his Wife*, John Murray, 1972
Bryant, Arthur, *The Age of Elegance*, Collins, 1950
  English Saga, Collins, 1940
Burghclere, *see* Gardner
Cavendish, Lady Frederick, *Diary of Lady Frederick Cavendish*, 2 vols, John Murray,
  1927
Cavendish, Georgiana, Duchess of Devonshire, *Extracts from Correspondence of*, ed.
  Earl of Bessborough, John Murray, 1955
Cavendish, Lady Harriet, *Hary-O: Letters of Lady Harriet Cavendish, 1796-1808*,
  ed. Sir G. Leveson Gower, John Murray, 1940
Cavendish, William George Spencer, sixth Duke of Devonshire, *Handbook of
  Chatsworth and Hardwick*, London, 1844
Cecil, Lady Gwendolen, *Life of Robert Cecil, Marquis of Salisbury*, 4 vols, Hodder and
  Stoughton, 1921-32
Cooper, Lady Diana, *The Rainbow Comes and Goes*, Hart-Davis, 1958
Cornforth, John, *Attingham Park*, National Trust Guide
Creevey, Thomas, *The Creevey Papers*, ed. John Gore, John Murray, 1948
Dawes, Frank, *Not in Front of the Servants*, Wayland, 1973
Egremont, *see* Wyndham
Farington, Joseph, *Farington Diary*, ed. James Greig, Hutchinson, 8 vols, 1923
Fedden, Robin, *Petworth*, National Trust Guide

Gardner, Winifred Anne Henrietta Christina, Baroness Burghclere, ed., *A Great Lady's Friendships, Letters to Mary, Marchioness of Salisbury, 1862-90*, Macmillan, 1933

A Great Man's Friendship, Letters of the Duke of Wellington to Mary, Marchioness of Salisbury, 1850-52, John Murray, 1927

Girouard, Mark, *Life in the English Country House*, Yale University Press, 1978

The Victorian Country House, Oxford University Press, 1971

Greville, Charles, *The Greville Memoirs, 1814-60*, ed. Roger Fulford and Lytton Strachey, 8 vols, Macmillan, 1938

Grosvenor, Loelia Mary, Duchess of Westminster, *Grace and Favour*, Weidenfeld and Nicolson, 1961

Hare, Augustus, *In my Solitary Life*, Allen and Unwin, 1953

Harrison, Rosina, *Gentlemen's Gentlemen*, Arlington Books, 1976

Henley, Dorothy, *Rosalind Howard, Countess of Carlisle*, Hogarth Press, 1958

Huggett, Frank E., *Life Below Stairs*, John Murray, 1976

Hussey, Christopher, *Attingham*, English Country Houses, 1956

James, John, *Memoirs of a House Steward*, Bury, Holt & Co., 1949

Kennedy, A.L., *Salisbury, 1830-1903*, John Murray, 1953

Keppel, George Thomas, Earl of Albemarle, *Fifty Years of My Life*, 2 vols, London 1876

Lees-Milne, James, *Attingham*, National Trust Guide, 1959

Lees-Milne, James, and Cornforth, John, *Chatsworth, Home of the Dukes of Devonshire*, Country Life, 1968

Lever, Sir Tresham, *The Herberts of Wilton*, John Murray, 1967

Lichine, Alexis, *Encyclopaedia of Wines and Spirits*, Cassell, 1975

Markham, Violet R., *Paxton and the Bachelor Duke*, Hodder and Stoughton, 1935

Milner, Violet Georgina, Viscountess, *My Picture Gallery, 1886-1901*, John Murray, 1951

Mitford, Mary Russell, *Our Village*, London, 1824

Oman, Carola, *The Gascoyne Heiress. Life and Diaries of Frances Mary Gascoyne-Cecil, 1802-39*, Hodder and Stoughton, 1968

Parker, R.A.C., *Coke of Norfolk*, Oxford, 1975

Pickering, A.M.W., *Memoirs*, 2 vols, London, 1903 (*see also* Stirling, A.M.W.)

Rose, Kenneth, *The Later Cecils*, Weidenfeld and Nicolson, 1975

Russell, G.W.E., *An Onlooker's Notebook*, John Murray, 1903

Collections and Recollections, London, 1903

Salisbury, *see* Gardner

Scott Thomson, Gladys, *Woburn and the Russells*, Pilgrim Press, 1956

Spencer-Stanhope, *see* Stirling

Stirling, A.M.W., *Coke of Norfolk and his Friends*, John Lane the Bodley Head, 1908

The Letter-bag of Lady Elizabeth Spencer-Stanhope, 1806-73, 2 vols, London, 1913

Odd Lives, P.R. Macmillan, 1959

Stirling Tales, London, 1961

Stuart, D.M., *The English Abigail*, Macmillan, 1946

Tayler, W., *Diary of W.T., Footman*, London, 1837

Thackeray, W.M., *Yellowplush Papers*, J.H. Roberts and Co., Sydenham, 1896

Thompson, F.M.L., *English Landed Society in the Nineteenth Century*, Routledge and Kegan Paul, 1963

Thompson, Francis, *A History of Chatsworth*, Country Life, 1949

Thynne, Daphne Winifred Louise, Marchioness of Bath, *Before the Sunset Fades*, Longleat Estate Company, 1951

BIBLIOGRAPHY

Trent, Christopher, *The Russells*, Muller, 1966

Turner, W.S., *What the Butler Saw*, Michael Joseph, 1962

Wellesley, Arthur, Duke of Wellington, *Wellington and his Friends*, ed. Gerald Wellesley, seventh Duke of Wellington, Macmillan, 1965

Wellington, *see* Gardner *and* Wellesley

Wells, H.G., *Experiment in Autobiography*, Gollancz, 1934

Westminster, *see* Grosvenor

Wyndham, John Edward Reginald, Baron Egremont, *Wyndham and Children First*, Macmillan, 1968

Young, G.M., *Victorian England: the Portrait of an Age*, Oxford University Press, 1960

Index

3